Michael Jackson

American Master

C. Mecca

Michael Jackson

American Master

CAM PUBLISHING - CALIFORNIA USA

Copyright 1996 by C. Mecca

10 9 8 7 6 5 4 3 2
First Edition

ISBN 0-9655174-0-3

Frontispiece: "Madonna on the Stairs"
by Michelangelo Buonaroti. Used by
permission of Scala Art Resource.

Photography: All photographs courtesy of
MJJ Productions, Inc.

Printed in Korea by Sung In Printing America, Inc.

Published in the United States of America by:
Cam Publishing
PO Box 550
Millbrae, CA 94030 USA

This book is dedicated to

Michael Jackson

and all the Masters

yet to be

"The world applauds the accomplishments;
The author applauds the man."

Table Of Contents

The Essence
Setting the Stage
Message to the Master
King of Pop

The Manifestation of Michael Jackson

The Master Confronts the Issues of the World

Photo Courtesy of MJJ Productions

The Essence

"He is a composite of the image that nature desires for every individual to attain..."
Bob Jones

The message of the ancient masters goes way back in the annals of time. They have their roots in civilization before the earthly appearance of the master of Christianity. The masters had the fortitude and wisdom to know that their life experience was not merely a personal journey, but a message for eternity. Such persons understood the ultimate earthly purpose of man was to impart his knowledge through his talent and philosophy for all mankind.

The development of their individual talent was necessary; but in order for it to be manifested in the physical world, it required the masters to know about the universal laws of which they were an integral part.

The Master. Where is he to be found in this generation? Would a Creator who had given the planet the gift of masters in the past suddenly let our contemporary world be without such a teacher? Would such a gift be denied, diminish, and finally become extinct so that people would be left without a living example? Are the multitudes floundering because they do not have a prime personage to emulate in their own lives?

Surely, the people of the earth would continue to need the teachings and examples of the master to continue to enhance their lives. Was man left to feign for himself without the teachings of a master?

Where is such a person who has the insight to draw on the whole scope of universal principles -- those precepts which include both the physical and spiritual ramifications of life? As history repeats itself, there certainly must be such a person present among our midst. History books can be explored to discover that many such people appeared in each of the previous generations. Research can teach of the artistry of such persons living in a past era. A person can further his understanding of the masters by studying the artistic forms of those rare and talented individuals who could see, comprehend and record the immensity of the creative resources of nature which reside within their being.

Who is the master for our generation? What is his message?

A woman had these very same questions, and she found the pathway to my office on May 13, 1994. Her message was unusual and different than most individuals who find their way to our door. She explained to me that she didn't really want me to actually do anything. She remarked that her mission was to write a book on a master of our generation. She said that, in her heart, she felt that she knew who this master is; she had done extensive research of the past masters and that all the qualifications pointed in the direction of Michael Jackson.

The woman mentioned that she would need permission to write such a book about Michael. Although this isn't the usual procedure these days, due to the subject matter she explained that she felt it was necessary. She would never attempt to write about another individual without his full consent.

She explained further that for the book to carry the proper message and be credible, it must be set apart from Michael's circle of friends and associates. The content had to be pure and untouched, and not influenced by other people; this, she felt, would assure that the intent remained true and pure.

Since she felt the contents had to be extremely accurate and honest, the author did make two requests. One, that I would review the completed manuscript; and two, that I would assist in revealing Michael's essence by donating the artistic material and introducing the master to the world by writing the foreword.

She believed that in the years of working and associating with Michael, I would, naturally, be the logical person to describe this talented, creative and diversified man. I have known Michael since the early stages of his career at Motown.

It was easy for me to accept such an invitation because, although Michael describes himself as being a very private person, he is also a very open, honest, caring and humble man. People should not find it necessary to search the minute personal aspects, events and actions of his life to discover his essence.

Michael Jackson's every act, his every word and deed, easily reveal the essentials of his character, and exhibit what a gifted person he truly is. He is also an extremely giving individual, as he continually shares his purpose with the world. Millions of people can feel his power and energy by listening to and witnessing his talent. No detail, no training, no practicing nor development, no creativity, is overlooked in illustrating the passion he has for life and all living creatures.

Michael is pure and innocent. He is also wise and shrewd with his intention of making this world a better place for mankind. When persons criticize his actions, lifestyle and beliefs, it causes him pain and remorse.

Such persons are missing the greatness and joy of his offerings to the planet. He desperately wants mankind to take advantage of the wonderment of nature and the uniqueness and purity that each child inherits at birth.

Some people attempt to look for the negative and the wrong, instead of the positive and the good, in another person. Michael Jackson has done exceedingly well in the past few years; and recent events have heightened his compassion for the world. People must understand that all of Michael's experiences have helped make him who he is, and reflect in the manner in which he presents his talent to the world. Such experiences add to, rather than detract from, the essence of his being and character.

Michael is truly a happy and content person. He has the innate ability to make the correct choices. He fell in love with a beautiful woman, and chose her as his wife. Such a woman is the perfect partner for him, and he a consummate husband for her. They have shared many years together.

Debbie Rowe is very familiar with the trials of being a member of a celebrity family. She understands what her husband needs to do to bring the messages of the master to the population. She knows that such a person as Michael must always have the freedom to bring his talent to the highest level of achievement of which he is capable. She is willing to give him his own time and space.

Michael makes decisions from both his heart and his intellect. Lately he has advanced his business empire by combining some of his assets and talent with the Sony Corporation. This move enhances both parties in their ability to bring forth more creativity for the public's enjoyment.

Many corporations are creating mergers in the realm of media which allow them greater expansion and development of network marketability. Many times, this can enhance the quality and diversification of their product.

This is not unusual in and of itself. What is astonishing is that one man joined forces with one of the largest corporations, not just in the entertainment industry, but in the world.

Michael Jackson sincerely loves everyone who shares the world as his home. He has spent his life developing his talent with the sole purpose of bringing joy, love, peace and understanding to his universal family through his music, lyrics, dance, and creative writing. His latest album, *HIStory, Past Present and Future Book 1*, and the messages in this book, both reveal some of the issues and possible solutions for the current conditions of our planet.

How would I describe Michael Jackson to you? I would start by describing him as a perfectionist, and a person who strives for excellence in everything he commits himself. He is a composite of the image that nature desires for every individual to attain by representing the goodness in life and in his fellow man. He is compassionate and sensitive. He is as strong as a rock. He is an example to follow for every human being who wants to make the very best of his or her life experience and to leave a part of their presence as a guide for future generations. Michael Jackson is exemplary as the master of our place and point of time on the planet.

This book can be one of the first stages in discovering the true essence of life. Its contents can appeal to every reader on a recreational level, yet advance the reader to a higher level of comprehension through studying the thought process of Michael Jackson.

– *Bob Jones*

Vice President
MJJ Productions, Inc.

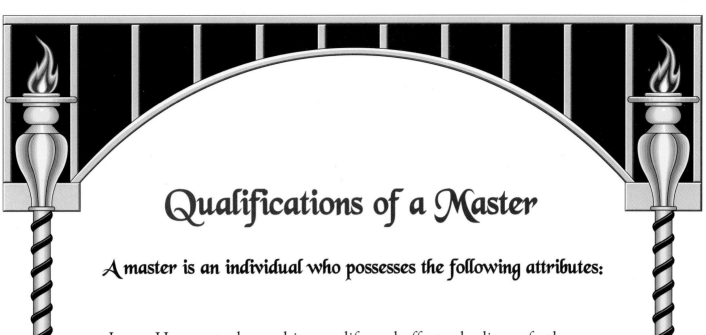

Qualifications of a Master

A master is an individual who possesses the following attributes:

I. Has control over his own life and affects the lives of others.

II. Develops his talent to the best of his ability.

III. Is concerned with the expansion of ideas and is not limited by arbitrary boundaries.

IV. Has a message or proposal in his life to share for the betterment of mankind.

V. Teaches and lives by example, which is in harmony with his beliefs.

VI. Is a philanthropist and a humanitarian by putting back into the environment in ratio equal to and that which he uses.

VII. Realizes that he is a result of nature.

VIII. Abides by and has a clear understanding of the laws of the universe.

IX. Enhances the world by his very presence.

X. Believes and uses the invisible power of intuition, inspiration and thought.

XI. Is a manifestor for our day and age.

XII. Has a thought process based on truth and, therefore, is free of making false decisions and judgments.

Photo Courtesy of MJJ Productions

Setting the Stage

The Masters! We read about the masters of past eras in reference books. We do research on them for term papers. We look at, revere and honor their work. We believe in our hearts that they made a place in the history of mankind. We set them apart as persons who are truly special by departing beauty and knowledge. These are the people who have led their generation to higher aspirations of every field of endeavor from the arts to the sciences.

Where are the masters? Did they appear in their robes and sandals for a brief moment in history, never to reappear? Are they a lost breed? Was their contribution to be solely for their generation and somehow not ever to surface again except in the annals of history? With the exception of their craft, what do we know about them? Are the masters present in this day and age?

The masters are present in abundant numbers today. In fact, they are present and prominent in every walk of life. The big question is, are we able to identify ourselves with their contributions to our generation? In today's world, due to technology, we can see and listen to the enlightenment they are departing and are willing to share with us on our televisions, CD players and radios. When we watch, listen and focus, we can apply the remedy in finding the answers to our own dilemmas and, perhaps, the world.

The book describes a chosen man who has conquered his goals and talents, and used his abilities to share his attributes with our generation. This book is in no manner a biography. Its purpose is to discover the elements and character of the masters' thought processes that led them to the attainment of their success. All of us are aware that it takes hard work and dedication in order to get ahead in the world in which we live.

These people have more intuition and fortitude. They dare to follow the direction their talent would lead them, which in most cases they are keenly aware of at an early age. They are the individuals who know how to make the best of the opportunities in which they can avail themselves. They also have the ability to compensate for any adversities.

This group of people we are going to discuss are those who make things happen by either jumping over hurdles or avoiding them altogether. They know how to create, develop, and expand their ideas. These are the individuals who know how to network with others. They seek out the help of those who can assist them in reaching their goals, and who are, in their own right, masters of expertise in their own areas.

Each goal that a master has just surmounted is merely a resting place on the climb to the next venture. To this select group, the planet is theirs and the sky is the limit. They take dominion over their space and make it work on their behalf.

Masters are those who have mastery over their own lives and combine their physical and spiritual self. The people of this select group reach the optimum of success in their own lives, and in turn make great contributions to the world.

Today, while our country is the most powerful in the world, it is suffering some of the same plights of less fortunate nations. It is a belief of the author that if we are able to learn some of the techniques of the masters, apply them in our own lives, and show responsibility for our own actions, we will find the solution to some of our own dilemmas. Then, on a larger scale, we can transfer the positive energy within ourselves to the outside environment. By doing this, we can take shared responsibility in solving some of the issues of our country and perhaps the world.

There are two areas where we can start in an attempt to obtain the answers. One is by perfecting ourselves and expanding our knowledge through the creative thinking process. Another might be not being so critical in our appraisal of others. If we can look, listen and study the masters and use them as examples in our own lives, we can learn some methods of reaching the success that we have envisioned for ourselves and the world. It is the hope of the author that this book will be in a prominent location in your collection of important reference materials.

If you have desire to have mastery over your own life, and that mastery is transmitted to the outside world, this is the opportunity to learn how to accomplish a life that is rich, satisfying and rewarding through your own personal discovery of the inherent traits and characteristics of those who have all the essential qualifications of a true master.

A Message To The Master

You were welcomed to a beautiful earthly home thirty eight years ago. You were guided through your young years by parents who nurtured your creativity. From the time that you became aware of the gifts of the planet, you were very inquisitive and you were different from most children of your age. You were given a talent and an indepth understanding of the world in which you reside. Although education played a dominant part in your early years, and you enjoyed attending school and playing with your brothers and sisters, your youth was channeled in another direction. The spiritual side in the form of music and dance began to consume most of your waking hours. For you, this was perfect, and the world stretched open its arms and embraced you.

The world extended its own knowledge. In doing this, it gave you the opportunity to travel, visiting the continents that make up the land where my people live and experience their life's purpose. While you were able to view the topography of the various countries that you traversed, you were able to study the diverse races, cultures, and lifestyles.

This isn't the usual way the average young person lives, grows and adapts to his environment. You were able to get a more comprehensive education. It was also very focused and evolved around your talent. You are one of the select people who have made the most of their life's experiences by their manifestations and contributions to their forms of art.

The universe is very much aware of the unselfish manner in which you used the innate talent that was bestowed upon you. It commends you for a job well done. My children who are sharing their life's journey with you received your messages. They have learned to develop their own talents; to realize the importance of having that talent reflect in all aspects of their lives.

You are now ready to add another phase to your life. This new stage is to elevate you to the select group of masters. You have grown in understanding. It was a painful time. The world operates on a sense of balance. Of course, you are quite aware of this principle as it is the main force that keeps all the planets and galaxies of the universe in place.

The balance in your life is exhibited by relying on the physical and spiritual components of your life, which complement one another. Experiencing both of these aspects will give you the rewards of peace and harmony beyond measure.

The true balance of your life will be present when you reflect on the recent events in your life. Try to incorporate such experiences in a positive manner which will enhance your being. This can be best accomplished by the purity of your intentions. Your master qualities will focus on the future by the lessons learned from the past. This is the manner in which the world advances as each experience is the cornerstone for the next encounter.

These experiences developed your understanding on how the populace may view the master. It serves as a constant reminder how fragile my children's comprehensions are of the events of the master's experience and the true pathway to growth and expansion.

It is of small consequence. The universe is willing to extend its arms and create an environment of love by providing a safe atmosphere in your home and society so that your creativity will thrive.

Sometimes, my children have not benefited from all the attributes of the master. They can easily lose their focus. It gets scattered when they concern themselves with unimportant facets of information that are not pertinent to the master's offering, and form opinions that are without a solid foundation.

Lately, the joining of the master and the populace has not been fully understood regarding the attributes of union. The close association between the public and the master can illustrate and enact one of the highest qualities of mastership. The joining of the energy of the master and his audience exhibits the basic foundation of the universe. The meeting of the master and his following combines two distinct groups displaying different needs into one purpose to make them a unit.

This is in perfect harmony with the teachings of universal law where two independent poles use their force to go in adverse directions and pull back to the center. This creates the equal balance by fulfilling the prime intention of enmeshment with each other.

The world always watches the actions and accomplishments of the masters. They are positive motivation for their lives. During your visit on the earth, you have exhibited the epitome of the masculine trait of expansion in all of your endeavors.

Displayed by the staggering number of people who delight in attending your concerts, the sharing of your talent will take you to the far corners of earth as you offer the results of your field of expertise in your particular contribution of art.

Sometimes, due to people's earnest desire to share the magnitude of your brilliance, they distort the meaning of your intentions. This creates a temporary imbalance of the spectrum of the two poles of your personal and public life. At this point, when the master relies on the invisible power of intuition, inspiration and thought, the two poles stabilize.

The invisible portion of the atmosphere will give you a clear and constant visual picture. In your heart, you will know what to think and do. This picture will be real, accurate and reliable. It is the primary characteristic that the master often applies in his interaction with his offering to the planet.

You have extended your talent, love, and gifts to the inhabitants of the planet, beyond human boundaries. You have transcended any records that can be easily digested by previous standards of measurement.

In their earnest desire to comprehend, the populace eagerly seek the answers. In doing so, they are following the usual method of searching for the answers in their physical environment. Strangely, they haven't found them. Surprisingly, they are not to be found in the familiar surroundings of the places of interest where they are looking.

The world needs a role model who has the solutions. The inhabitants need to know that the answers to the questions they are earnestly seeking are in the realm of the master's intuitive power and thought process.

As the world observes the lifestyle of the masters, they should adopt the positive motivation in their own lives. Sometimes, it isn't always easy for them to identify the true significance of the various events of the masters' experiences. To further assist them in their search, this book has been written.

The manner in which you have lived your life has been one of the major contributing factors to this book. It is one of the gifts from the planet. It is a way of letting you know that your accomplishments have been acknowledged. It is hoped that the message will serve as a comfort and guide, not only for yourself and the select group of present masters, but for all of the brothers and sisters who share their earthly home with you.

The universe will continue to keep the balance in your life by showering its nurturing components as an outward display of its acknowledgment. It will give you an assurance for your continued growth and happiness. You will be constantly aware of its presence and feel the warm characteristics as it embraces you with its beauty and protection.

It is paramount that you manifest all that you can be, as the horizons, possibilities, opportunities, and accomplishments are unlimited in the mind of the masters. The universe will support you by revealing its wish and dream for the master of this decade and the entrance of the twenty first century.

This gift, in the form of a book, is more than the accomplishments of a man. It transcends your childhood. It bypasses the title of the King who represents the leader in the particular field of his talent. It is about a very special person who has reached the highest position of attainment in one of the greatest countries of the world. You are entering into the select group of masters whose creative thought process and possible solutions of issues of the planet will become part of the history of our generation.

– An Instrument of Nature

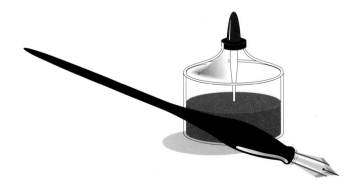

King of Pop

"The King of Pop." "The King of Pop." How many people have heard the chant? How many people can identify the person by such a phrase? It's used to describe a person who has preeminence over all others in his class. A person who bears such a title reigns superior over all others in a category. He is a monarch due to the primary reason that he holds a dominant position over others in his field of endeavor. Naturally, the person who holds this description is Michael Jackson and his dominion is music.

What makes a king? To be a ruler? To be superior? To have dominion? No doubt, all of these definitions could be suitable, but are they all inclusive in describing an individual of the stature of Michael Jackson? In studying, we are not limiting the title simply to pop, because that would limit the kingship down to one specific form of entertainment. In the case of Michael, the characteristics of a king encompass more than his creativity, stage persona, and musical expertise, as these traits exhibit the final results of years of training.

There are many entertainers who emulate superior qualities in their talent and none of them attempt to rule; perhaps they attempt to dominate, but certainly not rule. The world is full of very talented people who do not have the title of king prefacing their name.

What gives Michael this distinguished title? Of course, his accomplishments in the entertainment industry would be the most common answer. Everyone will unanimously agree that he certainly excels in the musical arena, but that isn't the only area of his expertise, because his creativity doesn't culminate with that one form of talent.

In studying this highly motivated individual, the reader will discover some of the underlying reasons that Michael Jackson has reached such attainment to be called "The King of Pop." The title is not only fitting in the field of entertainment, but in describing his own life.

In order to be a leader, head of a group or field, a person has to be knowledgeable, not only of the particular endeavor, but of all of the many other factors that make up the subject. It might be described as knowing all the components that are involved. Michael not only has to have a complete understanding of music, but of what appeals to his audience.

In order to be able to do this, he has to have a complete and comprehensive understanding of life in general. This entails knowing what the core, or essence, of life truly is; the needs, emotions, survival, or purpose of our existence which includes growth and expansion.

We know that to remain in top form takes practice and experimentation. It takes observation and studying to stay abreast in a particular field. It takes creativity and a certain amount of balance between many components of the natural or spiritual side, and having the ability to incorporate the material or physical aspects of life. To do this takes a highly motivated and dedicated individual, and one that is open to change and an innovative way of life.

To the author, people of this caliber are extremely rare and precious because they work unselfishly for the betterment of mankind and the planet. In truth, these people are not simply kings or queens, but masters. You see, kings are present for their own generation, but the teachings of the masters are forever.

Michael exhibits mastery quality in all areas of his life. His understanding and his techniques are timeless, just as the masters that he studied have affected and enhanced his own understanding of life. As a result of Michael's life, future generations will benefit, grow, and develop master qualities.

The Manifestation
of
Michael Jackson

Chapter 1:

Michael Jackson: A Master Speaks

"The greatest education is watching the masters at work."[1]
- Michael Jackson

No one individual exemplifies the twelve characteristics of the master in their entirety more than the man, Michael Jackson. No work on the masters would be complete or accurate without including him. He has such a special, rare, refreshing, and natural quality about him that he deserves to be the individual discussed in our book. One can observe these qualities by focusing on his lifestyle, his lyrics, and arrangements, but most of all by giving particular interest to the way he manifests.

An outstanding feature is his ability to share his purpose in life, both in his talent, and his desire to share and preserve the planet. In this regard, he is a profound teacher. Much has already been said, or written, about his record shattering concerts, his number one singles and albums, his numerous awards, his abundant wealth, his estate, his business empire, and his family.

What more can we possibly say in doing justice to this genuine and distinguished individual that is refreshing, new and timely? A lot! Since most of the books that have been previously written are predominantly concerned with his artistry and family, we are going to leave most of those factors alone. Most of the populace is relatively familiar with those remarkable accomplishments.

On the subject of Michael Jackson, let's learn how this master views life, the planet, and some of the contemporary issues facing our generation. This is by no means a psychological study, the primary reason being the author is not a therapist. To try to guess a person's thinking process, or even attempt to project further meaning to statements that a person has made in order to extract meaning, is dangerous. In fact, it is an invasion of his privacy to the highest degree.

This is one of the biggest problems people of celebrity status have. Michael made this point very clear on the television special, *Michael Jackson Talks With Oprah*. "Don't judge a person unless you have spoken to that person, one on one," he warns.

Michael is one of the easiest celebrities to observe mastership, due to the examples he uses when he communicates through his diverse mediums of song, dance, his Neverland Valley Ranch, his business acumen, but most of all, in the manner in which he speaks. Most people would respond, "Come on, this is a man of few words. He speaks very little." Now, this is an excellent point. This is one of the highest traits of a master.

Think about all of the previous masters who have graced our earth. How do they speak when communicating with the populace? Usually in parables. They give answers by telling short stories. They give examples as a means of drawing comparisons. They answer the original question by proposing another question to the listener.

Michael is an expert with this technique. Communication for Michael is apparent in the lyrics to his songs, especially those he has composed. He also has an indepth understanding of the universe which gives balance to his expression by the use of metaphors.

While we are not going into detail in mentioning his accomplishments, it is worth mentioning that he has received more awards than any other performer in the history of the entertainment industry. He has the biggest turnout on his concert tours; both in the number of countries he visits and the multitudes of fans attending his concerts. In Rome, Italy, he performed for 100,000 fans, and in England he performed for 137,000 fans -- and that's just two countries. Due to the excellence of his talent and his immense popularity, he received a fifteen million dollar commercial contract and a billion dollar entertainment contract.

While this may seem to be a staggering amount of money to the average person and his own earning power, a master realizes his earning capacity is always in direct ratio to his efforts and service he renders to the planet. An individual with Michael's talent and reputation can negotiate for large sums of money and can expect to receive the request. It is important to remember that to share his expertise requires him to spend equally large sums to bring the quality of his talent to the public, maintain his businesses, and maintain his lifestyle. Of course, he, too, must be able to enjoy the fruits of his labor.

He secured his place in history by having his name included in the Guinness Book of Records, not just once, not twice, but three times. In February, 1984 his *Thriller* album surpassed the forty million dollar sales mark, and he is the artist who won the most Grammys in a single year. One can also add the "Special Achievement Award," and as recently as 1993, "The American Legend Award" at the Thirty Fifth Grammy Award ceremonies. In May of the same year, he was off to Monaco to be acknowledged and honored by the world with other awards.

Who is this man called Michael Jackson whom we are discussing? Is he for real? Yes, he is a normal and successful human being. You see, his accomplishments represent only half of his individual assets; the other part of the man has to do with what he has learned and the sharing of his talent, not only with our country, but the world. He has given more world tours than any other performer to date. You may travel into another country and hear a foreign language, but you'll be able to understand Michael's name spoken quite clearly!

How does Michael do this and why is he a master of our time? It has to do with his belief system and how he manifests those beliefs and ideas. If we, too, can learn from the master, we can enjoy fulfilling lives. Every one of us has our own opinion of the world, and we can learn by observing how people perceive each other. Having a true friend is a wonderful experience. We can reveal the innermost parts of ourselves. We can share our joys and fears. We come to that special person in time of need, and he can do the same.

One such friend of Michael's is Elizabeth Taylor. She described her dear and close friend as one who is "least weird, highly intelligent, shrewd, intuitive, understanding, sympathetic, and generous."[2]. She also commented, "If anything, he's larger than life." She was referring to his artistry.

"Larger than life" is an accurate assessment of her perception of her friend. However, if Michael's talent is "larger than life," then so must be his comprehension of it. This response carries a weighty connotation and deserves much for us to contemplate in our own lives. In order for you to be larger than something, you have to either be a part of it or be compared to it.

A master sees himself as part of a process and therefore embraces it. The master observes and studies the scope of life and then has the ability to translate that knowledge to physical form by using his talent or position to let it travel to the outward perimeters of the planet. It's a type of true understanding and realizing that there are no boundaries in the external world; it's limitless.

"...I do love achieving goals. I love not only reaching a mark I've set for myself but exceeding it. Doing more than I thought I could, that's a great feeling. There's nothing like it. I think it's so important to set goals for yourself. It gives you an idea of where you want to go and how you want to get there. If you don't aim for something, you'll never know whether you could have hit the mark."[3a]

Photo Courtesy of MJJ Productions

Elizabeth Taylor's description reveals a great deal concerning her friend and gives us the characteristics which contribute not only to reaching his personal aspirations, but to his immense success in the physical world. Her adjectives of "highly intelligent, shrewd, intuitive, and understanding" are a winning combination. The use of intuitive power is one of the primary elements of a master's creativity.

Intuitiveness commences way down deep within us; it's a feeling. In common terms, we can call it a "hunch." When an artist acts upon it and nurtures it with his understanding, and sharpens his thought process, the feeling unfolds and is evident in physical form. As he acts upon his insights, he is able to clearly comprehend the character, the nature and subtleties of the inherent feeling or emotion of his intuition.

This, of course, takes a certain amount of sensitivity of knowing himself; otherwise, he is not aware of the stimulus and thus is not taking advantage of the involvement of the intuitive process which enables one to find innovative approaches to solutions.

Intuition generates a sense of purity for two specific reasons: (1) It operates in isolation from the cognitive side of the brain; and (2) Since it originates from this true part of our being, the invisible side, it is pure and untouched by outside influences which can give us a more clouded vision of what is natural or true.

How many times do we get an idea or inspiration, and in the next breath, tell ourselves, "Oh, I can't do that!" A master's response would be, "And why not?" The intuitive source of power can be used in solving some of the greatest problems we are facing in the world; it would harness the unique, creative, and original resources. When someone comes up with this type of idea, all of us will look at one another with a certain degree of puzzlement and ask one another, "Oh dear, why didn't we think of that before?"

This is a primary characteristic of a person of master quality. He does get an idea, and he does expand and act upon it. Michael acts on the vision of an idea. He then goes beyond the original concept and expands and enhances it, and gives it a new dimension. In doing this, he has a thorough and deep comprehension on how the advancement of mankind evolves.

"Pioneering new ideas are exciting to me".[3b]

Masters of yesteryear would do this all the time. They would take a basic philosophical concept and expand the principle to a higher plane into the spiritual realm. Michael explained that this is the true essence of art; the relationship between the material and the spiritual. All of the masters share this quality. They accomplish this by being cognizant of their surroundings, and then balancing them with the invisible or spiritual self. The masters give it physical form by using the modes of their talent to share with the rest of the world.

Michael exemplifies these characteristics in all of his endeavors. He understands these principles and applies them to all of his undertakings and efforts; not just his music, even though his music is his dominant medium. Here again, though, he applies the exact same principle in all areas of his life. He purchases a 2,700 acre piece of property and creates a Neverland Valley Ranch that looks as if it were a picture brought to life from a fairy tale. He takes a twenty-five room house, and remodels and decorates it, as if it is a representation of a palace fitting for kings and queens.

This isn't so unusual when he is the same person who takes the music video and changes its history by wondering what would happen, if instead of just having an artist singing a song, he acted out the song and extended it to tell a story and make a short film.

This changed the history of the music video. In his short film, based on the song *Black or White*, instead of simply seeing and hearing an artist, we can see Michael turn into a panther and back into Michael. We can witness a father blown out of the roof of his house and deposited in a terrain where Michael is dancing with natives, because the father had admonished his son for having his music too loud and the son set up his speakers in the living room and set the volume to the "Are you nuts?" stage.

All of this from just one song? No, there is more. How about dancing with the Russians or in front of a pharaoh and his queen? Or on a busy street? Expansion of creativity? Indeed!

It is surprising that the original version of this video was banned from TV. A master always has a message in his work. Through this short film he was showing the need for our society to abolish racism and discrimination. If you haven't had the opportunity or the experience of seeing any of Michael's videos, you might enjoy doing so, as they truly exemplify his talent, creativity, and artistry. You might begin with his newest short films from *HIStory: Past, Present and Future, Book 1*.

By creating the music short film, he also fulfilled another dream he had in life, and that was to make films and be an actor. He may have plans to do a major film. However, in the meantime, he uses his creativity, not only to enhance music videos, but to manifest a personal goal of his in a very innovative way through the use of expansion, and, of course, the use of his imagination and the intuitive self.

A master uses his creativity in numerous ways and takes every opportunity to illustrate his talent. Michael took advantage of providing the entertainment for Super Bowl Sunday on January 31, 1993, to use his exceptional talent and style. He turned the half-time period into a pageant; something that had never before been done so extravagantly, complete with fireworks and visual effects. Michael took the opportunity to address the crowd and television viewers about his hopes for a planet that reflects a common purpose of joy, understanding and goodness. He mentioned that no one should have to suffer; especially the children.

Michael's interview with Oprah Winfrey in February, 1993, viewed by ninety million viewers, gave them a lot of insight concerning the person that he truly is. Some people said that he did it for publicity. Whatever his reason was, it was an excellent decision on his part. You see, this person by the name of Michael Jackson was answering probing questions from Oprah. The surprising factor is that it didn't appear that we were listening to MICHAEL

JACKSON, the megastar, but simply to a kind, soft, well-mannered individual conversing informally in his home. The first question he was asked was whether or not he was nervous. He responded, "No, I never get nervous, no." His demeanor and body language reflected that to be true as he answered the question honestly.

It was mentioned that the questions were not discussed prior to the program. Whether they were or not is not a significant factor. Michael, no doubt, knew what the subject material would be, as the initial purpose of the interview was to put to rest many of the rumors that have been circulating around him for some time.

In any case, the prominent factor was the manner in which he answered the questions. He was serene, soft, and relaxed. His body language, voice, and speech rate were in sync. The comfortable delivery was apparent in his posture, and the positioning of his hands, which were placed restfully on top of a crossed leg. When he wanted to emphasize a point, his hand would go to his chest, or he would point his index finger, and then his hand once again would return to his lap. There were no stiff, erratic movements. His eyes reflected sensitivity and focus, but nothing, absolutely nothing, could compare to his smile and occasional chuckle in response to some of the inquiries.

This is a prime example of the conduct of the masters in an appearance before their audience. They depict confidence and respect in their softness and relaxed manner. They do not let their adrenaline flow, or use the flame of their emotions to make a point during their presentation.

Michael discloses a great deal about his philosophy, priorities, and the fault in giving credence to inconsequential points, thereby missing the main idea and/or the true substance of the topic.

A master knows how to ask the correct questions to increase his knowledge on a particular subject. The relationship between the master and the student's clarity is in asking the correct questions. Since there are many components in the scope of things, asking a specific question is limiting the master.

In order for the student to learn a subject in its entirety, he must know the scope of the topic before he can narrow it down to the specifics. The master cannot answer the question by departing knowledge unless he can adequately describe the material and its ramifications. A true master lets the student arrive at the proper conclusion through studying or analyzing. A master is always eager to speak on his craft, and less eager to discuss unrelated subjects.

Michael understands this technique extremely well. He exhibited this method when he explained that he was a great fan of art. He said that he loved Michelangelo. In true master form, he said, "If I had a chance to talk or read about him, I would want to know what inspired him to become who he is. The anatomy of his craftmanship, not who he went out with last night or why he sat out in the sun so long."

This technique was also illustrated when the subject came up about the color of his skin and the fact that it has become lighter in recent years. He was very sincere and showed his sensitivity in his answer. His hand went to his chest, his eyes watered, and his voice wavered when he was asked if he bleached his skin. Michael remarked that he didn't know of anything such as skin bleaching. He explained that he has a skin disorder that destroys the pigmentation of the skin. He said that he doesn't understand it, and that his father said that it came from his side of the family. He then said that it leaves blotches on the skin and that using makeup evens out his skin.

He says that it hurts him when people make up stories about him, inferring that he doesn't like to be who he is. Then, in true master form, he said, "Let's reverse it. What about all the millions of people who sit out in the sun to become darker, to be other than they are. Nobody says anything about them".

Michael's expertise at answering questions, and his ability to educate the viewers by bringing their opinions to a higher level, was apparent in his response to many questions. He was asked if he wanted a white child to play him in a commercial. The answer as to whether he did or didn't want a white child was not the outstanding feature of his reply. What was outstanding was that while he was asked a specific question about a commercial, he expanded his answer to show how he feels about himself.

To show his deep feeling in answering, once again, he lightly, but firmly, hit his chest with his hand when he said,

> "Why would I want a white child to play me? I am a Black American. I am proud to be a Black American. I am proud of my race. I am proud of who I am. I have a lot of pride and dignity in who I am."

This one declaration tells his audience how he perceives himself, his heritage, and his country. It carries a message that is one of expansion and not limitation. All people, all over the world, heard this statement. He gave strength, not weakness, to his race. He doesn't simply accept who he is, but carries pride and dignity with who he is and his ancestral background.

What a beautiful way to assess one's life. This one statement can do wonders in breaking down barriers and excuses for success. A master has the innate ability of saying a lot with a few words. However, those few words have the means of changing the world. While many people want to cast the blame of their frustrations on something other than themselves, a master speaks using himself as an example or a neutral object. Michael does not criticize anyone. He uses all of his being to his advantage and not his detriment. He is honored by being a member of his race and his country and who he is. This is a powerful statement in finding success.

In order to succeed, a person has to use the positive and bypass anything negative. To take what nature has designed for a purpose in order to attain the maximum fulfillment, and not use it for that specific purpose, is not in harmony with nature's gift. Everything the world contains is part of oneness. If we don't comprehend this relationship, we remain stuck and no progress is made. The universe stresses oneness. Nature does not create anything superior to another. All elements are equal and are made in perfect manifestation according to their purpose and environment. To demean one's function, and the attributes of that creation, is to deny the Divine.

This being true, all human beings are the same. The differences are, in the larger scope of things, minor. Those small differences, our physical features, were necessary due to the origins of our heritage. The survival of each particular race was dependent upon them.

When man was created, he was created from the same source. Every human being has the same internal structure. The solution to racism is to accept and hold in high regard the wonderment of that creation; its sameness, and its uniqueness, which is manifested by our talent and creativity.

In our country's beginning, there were many misgivings in the understanding of the human race. Unfortunately, we can't go back and do things differently. The past is over and part of history. It has been completed. It is over. Done!

What we can do is to think in the terms of a master and turn our eyes toward expansion. We cannot move forward at the very same time we are moving backward, as this destroys our unity. Since we cannot change the past, we can learn from the failures of the previous generations and accentuate all that is positive. We do this when we appreciate and revere what all of us have in common and unite with our oneness. We know that in truth, we are all sisters and brothers.

Michael wrote about the importance of being One with the Creator in *The Dance*. How profound! This master realizes and shares, through his message, that he has become one with everything that exists. All of us are part of the oneness, the Creator.

Michael's words also illustrate the bond between the giver and the receiver. The Creator gives the essentials and the ability to create or use our talent. We, in turn, take the gift of our talent and create something innovative and give it out to the planet, which warmly and graciously receives the offerings of our labor. This is an important concept, as it transcends every area in our lives.

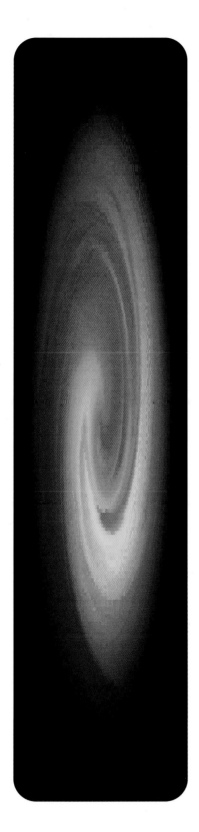

The Dance

"Consciousness expresses itself through creation.
This world we live in is the dance of the creator.
Dances come and go in the twinkling of an eye but
the dance lives on. On many occasions when I am
dancing, I have felt touched by something sacred.

In those moments, I felt my spirit soar
and become one with everything that exists.
I become the stars and the moon.
I become the lover and the beloved.

I become the victor and the vanquished.
I become the master and the slave.
I become the singer and the song.
I become the knower and the known. I keep on
dancing then it is the eternal dance of creation.

The creator and the creation merge into one
wholeness of joy. I keep on dancing ... and
dancing and dancing, until there is only ....

The Dance".[4]

Equally significant is our understanding of this reciprocal relationship. The receiver gets a gift from the giver, and uses, develops, and expands it. In like manner the receiver, in turn, gives the expansion of his gift out to others so that they can receive the results of the giver. This relationship can interchange back and forth; to and fro.

The author has written about how Michael feels about himself, his race, and his heritage. All of us use the innate ability of our talent to tell others how we feel concerning the elements of the outer world of our environment. If our beliefs are a true and honest representation of our self, they are going to be consistent in our expressions and actions in the physical world. Michael's statement regarding his heritage is in harmony with his core beliefs, and reflected in the lyrics of his song, *Black Or White.*

Michael mentions that he has a lot of pride and dignity in who he is. This is an essential trait of a master, and a reason that Michael has the phenomenal results that he has obtained using his creativity. It also denotes that he has very good self-esteem:

"I believe we are powerful, but we don't use our minds to full capacity. Your mind is powerful enough to help you attain whatever you want."[6]

In the last decade, we have heard a lot about the term "self-esteem." Like most characteristics, it must be used and kept in proper perspective. We can't produce to the best of our ability if we do not acknowledge or realize our own empowerment. We have to feel worthy of our ability to create. If we don't believe this about ourselves, we are operating in the realm of limitation. We become prisoners of our sense of scarcity instead of abundance.

The quality of good self-esteem radiates from within and flows outward in our interaction with others. It has a peaceful, quiet, spiritual feeling within the individual, and depicts confidence. Like any quality, it can be misunderstood and, therefore, misused.

Black or White

"See, it's not about races
Just places
Faces
Where your blood
Comes from
Is where your space is
I've seen the bright
Get duller
I'm not going to spend
My life being a color

Don't tell me you agree
with me
When I saw you
Kicking dirt in my eye
.......I said if
You're thinkin' of
Being my brother
I don't care if you're
Black or White."[5]

One of the most common misuses of self-esteem is when it is associated with the use of power, which has to do with control, force, or the ego. Self-esteem is an inner trait which, as the word implies, has to do solely with the self.

"If you don't believe in yourself, who will? I think of it as they try to get what you call mentality. If it doesn't require you to stretch, to grow, I don't believe in that."[7]

Another example of Michael's understanding of the qualities of a master is found in his answer to the question, "What do you know for sure?" He responded simply, "Oh, I know nothing for sure. I am still learning."[8]

This remark divulges one reason that Michael is considered so intelligent. An intelligent person not only realizes what he knows, but is cognizant of what he doesn't know. It is said that only a fool thinks he knows everything.

Michael is very well educated. He had a private tutor who taught him not only the basics, but about the countries his family visited. He saw the cultural value of each different country he visited while they were on tour. He was exposed to the great classics of literature. Michael was taught about the great artists by Diana Ross. His love and his appreciation for these forms of art are apparent by the paintings that adorn his walls, and his library shelves are full of the classics.

He also has the insight to have associates to assist him in the operation of his business empire, to assist him in his music ventures, and to help maintain his home. To the average person, this could be mind boggling. All these people are part of the whole, and must depict the attributes of their fearless, tireless, and highly motivated employer.

In living in harmony and peace within ourselves, we can put these feelings out into the world to circulate. There is no better way to get more of what we want than by putting what we desire into circulation for the benefit of others. Whatever it is, release it to develop, grow and expand. Anything! Peace, happiness, money, thoughts, talent. Anything!

However, remember that negativity, of any source, will also manifest at the same rate. America is one of the greatest and richly blessed countries in the world -- in the world. It has been said by many of the most successful people of our land, "If you can't make it in America, you can't make it anywhere."

So why are we facing so much difficulty? We are putting our emphasis in the wrong place. Instead of spending time on the negative, put that energy on the positive and cultivate the good, not the bad.

> "...I am fascinated by the concept of revenge. It's something I can't understand. The idea of making someone 'pay' for something they've done to you or that you imagine they've done to you is totally alien to me."[9]

Where we put our thoughts and energy is what becomes a reality, and what we see and think becomes real to us. What we are looking for is always what we will find. If we see goodness in having empathy for our fellow man, we will see goodness in our endeavors, and that goodwill will manifest itself a hundred times over.

Life operates on a sense of balance. It works in earnest to maintain that balance. If you want to concentrate on the negative, the world will work overtime to create that balance in your life. It behooves one to be very careful with one's thoughts. That's where it all begins. One single thought placed in the consciousness can change the destiny, not only of a single person, but of mankind. A master knows the power of this principle.

Michael's single response to a simple question has a motivational message for anyone. With a slight variation, due to our diverse cultural backgrounds, people all over the world could repeat the passage daily, "I am proud of my heritage. I have a lot of pride and dignity in who I am." In thinking in this manner, we can all rise to be of master quality in our own lives because these are the thoughts of a true master.

The world in which we live, for the large part, is consistent. People change and so does their understanding of the world. We are becoming more and more sophisticated at an accelerated rate due primarily to the advancement of technology. Our likes and dislikes are changing, and so is our lifestyle. We are searching for a deeper meaning and understanding for our lives. Our tastes are changing; we are into a more healthy way of eating and into exercise. What is news today is old news tomorrow. What we used to discard, we save and what we used to save, we now discard.

The world is always ready and waiting for a new, better, or more efficient way of doing things. It is always searching for a deeper understanding of our life and purpose; a certain kind of intensity, and even restlessness. A master is subject to advancement in the form of taking a challenge. Michael knows that the search for knowledge is ceaseless and, at the same time, it is invigorating.

Photo Courtesy of MJJ Productions

Chapter 2:

The Master Reaches for Perfection

"A perfectionist has to take his time."
- Michael Jackson

Michael shows the manner in which he manifests mastership not only in terms of his talent, but in his physical environment as well. One of the characteristics of a master is to attempt to reach a quality of perfection not only in the development of his intrinsic abilities to be expressed in his talent, but in maintaining consistency in all of the areas in which he surrounds himself. Michael believes that,

> "A perfectionist has to take his time; he shapes, he molds, and he sculpts that thing until it's perfect. He can't let it go before he's satisfied; he can't."

> "...You work that thing till it's just right. When it's as perfect as you can make it, you put it out there. Really, you got to get it to where it's just right; that's the secret."[10]

A true perfectionist is not one who simply reaches perfection in one area of his life, but in all endeavors. A perfect example of this is Michael's Neverland Valley Ranch in Santa Ynez, California. The name aptly applies as it is very unlikely that one would ever find, or see, another location of equal stature. It truly is a dream place because it has given physical form to the dreams that Michael wanted to incorporate on the grounds of his estate.

Our homes should be considered sacred. It is the one place where we can reveal who we are without criticism. It is the place where we have the opportunity to plan and dream about our future. It is also the place that we can lay the foundation to execute those dreams in the form of goals, and then make the commitment to fulfill those dreams.

The master, in manifesting, uses all the available tools and concepts, and expands and elaborates them in order to come up with something innovative. All of us have seen and visited amusement parks, frequented zoos, played video games, and attended performances at theaters. The primary distinction with Michael is that all of these aspects of life are on one piece of property.

While the grounds of Neverland Valley Ranch reveal the interests of its owner, the inside of his home reveals his personality. Viewers fortunate enough to have seen the Oprah Winfrey interview saw a fraction of one of his rooms. It was enough, however, to see the character of his home. The objects and decor describe a great deal about what is important to the occupant through the color scheme, the books, the paintings, and the artifacts.

The outstanding feature of Neverland Valley Ranch is not just what it contains, but the creativity in the layout and the arrangement, down to the minutest details, including the spotless way the grounds and equipment are maintained.

Pictures of the property in Life magazine's article depict beautifully manicured lawns and pathways lined with yellow marigolds. The article also gives us more of a view of the amusement park, complete with bumper cars and small colorful golf carts to get to the far reaching corners of the land. The property is full of statues from Peter Pan. At night, the article tells us that the trees are lit with tiny white lights. It must be breathtaking!

One of the features viewers saw in the interview with Oprah Winfrey was Michael's theater, which is spacious and beautiful. Here, again, is attention to detail; the custom red seats and the large stage adorned with an oversized Oscar. Oprah Winfrey commented that, "One must be very caring about children to include them in his architecture by having two suites with windows facing the stage, complete with a hospital bed, so that children too ill to sit in the theater can enjoy the latest films, cartoons and videos".

In the life of a master, daydreaming and fantasy are some of the crucial aspects of his creativity. The sprawling property of Neverland is an outward display of how this master has the originality to act and fulfill those dreams. In commenting on the magnificence of the estate, Michael says, "This is pretty much how I imagined it".[11]

Masters always find, use or create an environment conducive to their work. It may be a spot where they can meditate, dream or become one with the universe. It may be sitting on the ground in front of a brook, or on the sand near the ocean; in the backyard, sitting in a lawnchair under the shade of a tree, or by the pool, sipping an ice cold beverage.

Michael has the perfect surroundings at home to nurture his creativity. We know that he has a great love of literature and that when he is in his study, he can feel the presence of every book. In his backyard there are amusement rides. Michael admits that on those nights, when he is alone on the ranch, he samples ride after ride, reaching for the stars, all by himself. He does it, he says, "All the time".[12]

Simply relaxing by enjoying recreation in the form of video games, watching cartoons, and the companionship of family and friends in the sharing of ideas and viewpoints, are special for Michael. Naturally, if this master should find all this too limiting, the world is at his disposal, ready and willing to embrace him.

Why does this master manifest in such a manner? There could be many possible reasons. As for such attention to detail, we might look to a few prominent mentors of Michael. One that people like to overlook is his father. Although he was overly strict ("Even a look would scare you", said Michael), he was a perfectionist when it came to all of his sons' talent. Berry Gordy took the boys' careers under his wing when they were under contract at Motown.

> "Berry insisted on perfection and attention to detail. This was his genius. Then and later I observed every moment of the sessions where Berry was present, and never forgot what I learned. To this day, I use the same principles. Berry was my teacher, and a great one."[13]

Another great influence in Michael's life was Walt Disney. Michael explains that Berry Gordy and Walt Disney were alike because both of them kept on top of their craft. We learned of Michael's feelings toward Mr. Disney when he was going to do Captain EO. He explained at a meeting at the studio,

> "...Walt Disney was a hero of mine and I am very interested in Disney's history and philosophy.." [14]

> "I wanted to do something then that Mr. Disney himself would have approved. I had read a number of books about Walt Disney and his creative empire, and it was very important to have things as he would have."[15]

When the Jackson boys were playing the chitlin's circuit, Michael had his opportunity to watch, study and incorporate the movements and style of James Brown. By Michael's description of him, one need not wonder why James Brown had such an influence. Michael writes,

> "Most of the time I'd be back stage...my brothers would be upstairs eating and talking, and I'd be down in the wings, crouching real low, holding on to the dusty, smelly curtain and watching the show. I mean, I did watch every step, every move,

Photo Courtesy of MJJ Productions

every twist, every turn, every grind, every emotion, every light move. That was my education and my recreation."

"His whole physical presence, the fire coming from his pores, would be phenomenal. You'd feel every bead of sweat on his face and know what he was going through. I've never seen anybody perform like him. Unbelievable, really. When I saw somebody that I liked, I'd be there. James Brown, Sam and Dave, the O'Jays -- they all used to work with the audience. I might have learned more from watching Jackie Wilson than from anyone or anything else. All of this was a very important part of my education."[16]

This is a learning technique that masters use. They take every opportunity to learn from their environment. In giving or receiving information, they use the value of an example, and even more important, they incorporate the example into their being. There were people in Michael's life like Sammy Davis Jr., and Quincy Jones, and dancers such as Gene Kelly and Fred Astaire. These stars are legends in their own right, and they are masters in their fields.

One of the best ways to learn is from the examples of others. Michael would stand in the wings of the stage and increase his knowledge. People who share the same interests associate with one another and give each other feedback. They also share one another's success as they know how difficult it is to reach the epitome of their craft; the devotion, commitment and the sacrifice of self.

Another reason Michael manifests his talent in the manner in which he does is that he is being true to himself. A master, above all, is sincere; what he manifests is what he is. People have attempted to project their opinions and reasoning in giving their assessment of Michael. For example, one reason for Michael's love of cartoons and video games, people have said, is that he missed out on them in his childhood. This also justifies his love and association with children. Michael agrees by saying, "This is very true." However, if you understand the actions, you can understand the person.

Michael does live in this lifestyle because he missed out on having a normal childhood, but there is more. It is one of his purposes in life to bring happiness into the lives of the terminally ill or disadvantaged children. His lifestyle also spurs a part of his creativity. Last, but most important, it is a diversion and creates a balance for what could be a very stressful life.

Some people believe that in returning to some of these activities, Michael became stuck and remained in a childlike mode. In describing himself, Michael feels that he is a musician who is, incidentally, a businessman. Michael is an expert in the field of business. He purchases the rights to the musical accomplishments of many popular artists, including the Beatles and Sly Stone. He enhanced the availability of part of his musical library by merging with Sony. This extended the ownership of his rights to many more musical artists. He produces new talent under his own MJJ record label. Michael has created several corporations, one of which is the Heal The World Foundation. In this endeavor, he has the assistance of the former United States President, Jimmy Carter.

This corporation works in three areas: (1) The immunization of children; (2) A Big Brother/Big Sister mentor program; and (3) A program on drug abuse. This effort illustrates a component of master quality: To live life in your own way, according to your conscience. These accomplishments take more than a child's rationale.

However, knowing part of the story, or singling out one aspect and using that one aspect to be all-inclusive, does not give an accurate picture. A master lives his life in a manner which is comfortable and satisfying to him. He is not concerned with what other people think about his lifestyle. In keeping with this characteristic of a master, Michael complies beautifully.

Equally important, a master is concerned with the care and beauty of the environment. Again, he excels! His estate is picture perfect. Michael says,

"I love daydreaming. I spend most of my time daydreaming."[17]

A master is generous and helpful with his wealth to people who can benefit from his services. In the following, Michael described a purpose that is paramount to the function of Neverland. At intervals, he plays host for terminally ill children. He recalled a fond memory, "...we had a household of baldheaded children. They all had cancer. One little boy turned to me and said, "This is the best day of my life." You just had to hold back the tears."[18] He still has more ideas for the ranch, which will include another area devoted to disadvantaged childrenm.

A master always puts his whole self into his manifestation. In doing this, his purpose originates from the inner core of his being. It includes his deepest feelings and emotions, and then appears in the physical realm through his ability to incorporate it into his thought process.

Michael's deep concern for AIDS was brought to the forefront when he spoke at the 52nd Presidential Inaugural Ball on behalf of AIDS and his friend, Ryan White, who died from the disease shortly after his eighteenth birthday. Michael made the introduction to his song in a very personal and heartfelt manner. He spoke of his friend and his close association with him, telling the audience that he wanted Ryan's life to have meaning beyond his passing.

After making a request that President-Elect Clinton and his administration commit the needed resources to eliminate the disease, he broke into the song, *Gone Too Soon.* He dedicated the song to Ryan. The lyrics are beautiful, and the use of metaphors to describe the short duration and frailty of life, and its comparison to nature, have a spiritual quality.

The performance of this star will remain in the hearts and the memory of the audience for a long time. If Michael wanted the memory of Ryan White to remain in our hearts, he couldn't have found a more effective way. There was a sense of oneness between the performer, his surroundings and the audience. The master of ceremonies barely completed the introduction of Michael when the audience stood up and started clapping.

Gone Too Soon

"Like a comet
Blazing 'cross the evening sky
Gone too soon

Like a rainbow
Fading in the twinkling of an eye
Gone too soon

Shiny and sparkly
And splendidly bright
Here one day
Gone one night

Like the loss of sunlight
On a cloudy afternoon
Gone too soon

Like a castle
Built upon a sandy beach
Gone too soon

Like a perfect flower
That is beyond your reach
Gone too soon

Born to amuse, to inspire,
to delight
Here one day
Gone one night

Like a sunset
Dying with the rising of the moon
Gone too soon

Gone too soon."[19]

Michael was introduced as being of entertainment royalty; that his credentials as an artist are unsurpassed, that he is a person who has a deep commitment to the future of the planet and the children of the world. As the title, "King of Pop", was being mentioned, it was overcrowded by the applause. However, when Michael began speaking and singing, there wasn't another sound in the auditorium.

A master always claims his space; it's his, and the results of that space are how he chooses to use it. Michael owns his space, and it willingly succumbs to him. His performance was moving. It was a wonderful experience to see one single person be in command, displaying such ease in his delivery. Michael has commented that the stage is home for him, and that he is most comfortable when he is performing. This was apparent.

The short film, *Dangerous*, illustrates *Gone Too Soon* by showing Ryan in memorable scenes of his life. There is one scene where Michael is walking with Ryan across a bridge. It was a cold day; the two had on jackets and their hands were in their pockets. You could tell that they were talking, and Michael pointed to something that he wanted Ryan to see.

From viewing the segment, it is apparent why there was such a close tie between the two of them. Ryan was a soft, sensitive human being, and he took pleasure in enjoying the simple aspects of his life. Why that one scene on the bridge had such an impact on this viewer was not difficult to ascertain. There was a super megastar walking with his young friend alone, together, away from the glare of a public image, enjoying quiet moments and the beauty of a natural landscape.

It was the author's desire to mention Ryan White because it is a wish of Michael's to have Ryan's memory remain. However, Ryan has done that individually, by himself. He, too, is deserving of, and has earned the honor of, being called a master in his own right. In the short time he was on the planet, he lived his life to the fullest, and we can learn by his example. He also educated us on how we should accept all people, regardless of their position or condition.

Ryan taught the world how to take an unpleasant experience, turn it around, learn from it, and continue on and concentrate on the positive side of life and living. He also taught us that an experience has nothing to do with time. The sum of one's experiences has to do with the quality of the use, and the knowledge that is gained from those experiences, not one's duration.

In May of 1996, Michael's request to President Clinton was fulfilled. The Ryan White Bill was enacted, providing $350 million for AIDS research. It gives the author much pleasure in ranking Ryan White among the masters. It was so easy to do, to recognize the attributes of the masters in Ryan. It is hoped that Ryan knows that he fulfilled his purpose in his short journey here with us, and now he should be happy and content.

Michael has a reputation as a philanthropist, and is one of the greatest humanitarians of our generation through sharing his talent and his fortune. He has given huge monetary gifts to individuals as well as charities. His generosity to benefit children is well known.

He established the Michael Jackson Burn Center with the $1.5 million he received from Pepsi. He has donated the proceeds of tours to the service of children. He has purchased and paid for medical equipment for the children of families who couldn't afford the costs, and he has even paid for the funerals of children who have met an untimely death through riots. Michael has made personal appearances to schools where students have had the unfortunate experience of witnessing the deaths of their schoolmates shot by a mad gunman. And we already mentioned the concern and love he showers on the terminally ill or disadvantaged young people. There is no one who understands more that such children are experiencing suffering way beyond their present years of life on the planet.

One may ask the reasoning for such generosity. A master understands that he should give back to the planet in direct ratio to his prosperity, and practices the principle of helping people who are less fortunate than himself. By doing this, nature appreciates, rewards and honors his donation.

Photo Courtesy of MJJ Productions

In return, he finds his life manifesting more of the abundance in the same likeness and proportion. A master also understands the reasoning behind the manifestation of our current problems. He sees the solution to be in giving our children a better life. He believes that many children, like himself, are robbed of their childhood. In children, Michael sees their innocence as they view the world as being something magical and mysterious.

In working with gang members for *Beat It*, he came to understand their position, and the underlying reason for some of their behavior:

> "I came to realize that the whole thing about being bad and tough is that it's done for recognition. All along, these guys wanted to be seen and respected. They're rebels, but rebels who want attention and respect. Like all of us, they just want to be seen. They were wonderful to me -- polite, quiet, supportive. After the dance numbers, they would compliment my work. It was nothing like acting. They were being themselves; the feeling you got was their spirit."[20]

Michael has illustrated this principle by taking people on shopping sprees, or by shopping for toys for children in the countries that he is visiting while on tour. He will visit a local "Toys 'R' Us" store and come out with shopping carts filled over the brim with toys, video games, videos and the like. He'll shop privately with a young friend, and tell him to pick out whatever he likes, while he is doing likewise.

Some people look at this lavish spending as spoiling these young recipients. A master might look at it quite differently. First, he may truly enjoy the act of giving. It might give him great satisfaction to see the joy, delight and appreciation from the receiver. Second, he can believe in circulating his wealth, both in giving to the child, and next, putting a portion of his effort in the form of money into the service of others. Third, he might be teaching the young through example that by sacrificing early in life and keeping in focus with a goal, when the right time comes, they will reap the benefits of their efforts. Last, the more willing one is to withhold instant gratification, the better the enjoyment and the less sacrifice that will later have to be made as one's position in life will be rooted and strong.

The developing of talent and the sharing of the result of that talent is a very rudimentary concept; one that a true master thoroughly understands. The sharing of talent by the use of labor is exhibited in two forms by the giver and receiver. It is displayed in the use of the talent, which reflects in a form of service and in symbol, which we commonly give the name, "money".

Few people see the relationship in this pure form. They separate the two, calling the labor "work" or "service", and seeing the money as payment. In truth, money is a mode of exchanging the results of labor. It is a form of advanced bartering. In more primitive times, a rancher would take his wares to a neighbor in exchange for something he wasn't manifesting himself. Instead of taking a chicken to the general store in exchange for material, we bring money or a credit card to the retail store. It is still an exchange of labor for service.

Let's examine how Michael exchanges his talent in the form of service and labor, which results in the equal symbol of money. The audience gives a portion of their labor in the form of purchasing tickets. In modern times, a master imparts knowledge which enhances the planet in the form of service and in the equal form of labor. We have already discussed his humanitarian efforts, and how he gives beauty to the physical world. Now, let's turn our attention specifically to concerts.

A master uses his talent to depart information before an audience. The type of means, the number of people, or the type of subject material will vary and is of small consequence. Corporate structures have their board meetings; universities have their professors; schools have their teachers; churches have their ministers; and homes have their parents. Michael has his stage and fans.

A master brings the total sum of his experience, knowledge and training to his audience when he feels that the timing and expertise is in harmony with the message which he wishes to convey. The segment that is going to receive the gift of the master has to be ready, willing and able to receive his offering.

In the case of Michael, the excitement of the fans begins years prior to the performance. They have purchased his music and they dream of having the opportunity to see him perform live. For many, simply being able to be in his presence would be fulfilling a fantasy.

They resolve the conflict of his schedule of appearances versus their own obligations. The most difficult task is being able to purchase tickets. The question in their minds is if they are going to be able to get a glimpse of, or even identify, the small figure on stage. Not everyone is able to have front row accommodations.

The day finally arrives for the fans to prepare for the concert. This is no small feat in itself. One must find transportation and parking, then usually a long walk to the arena. At the designated entrance, we then experience long lines and an equally long wait. Upon entering the location, the real excitement commences. There are many merchandising concessions exhibiting mementos as a symbol of the experience that we have waited, perhaps years, to see. There are stands where we can quench our thirst, or grab a bite to eat. We may even be fortunate enough to locate the restrooms because, already, it has been a very long day!

Looking for and finding our place to view the performance takes time, but the excitement is increasing. We can hardly believe that the event we have so much waited for is about to happen. We share our excitement with neighboring guests, and exchange information about the performer, who is just about ready to make his physical appearance before our very eyes.

We are becoming more aware of the reality of the situation when we see members of the performer's entourage. Displaying badges identifying themselves, they are seen making last minute preparations as everything has to be perfect in every detail. The moment that we have been waiting for is just about ready to begin. When the suspense is at its pinnacle, the mouth is dry, and the stomach is tied up in knots, the performance of our lifetime is becoming a reality. The dreams, the hopes, the desires, are going to happen in a minute, a second... now!

"We have something we want to tell you. The opening was so dramatic and bright and captured the whole feeling of the show. When the lights came on and they saw us, the roof would come off the place."[21]

Whatever transpires in the first few minutes of the concert will be spectacular and breathtaking, for it will set the mood for the rest of the performance. In those very first few seconds, it's difficult to concentrate as we don't know where to focus our attention in trying to see where the performer is going to appear on stage. Is he going to appear high on a stairway, or come from the side? Is he going to be encased with a group of dancers? Where to focus? We hear clapping and screaming, and look -- there he is!

A master knows the importance of setting the proper atmosphere. In order for people to get a message, they have to be in the proper frame of mind. The most effective technique is to set the mood. It makes the mind receptive to gaining increased knowledge, and helps the audience to focus.

Michael is the creator of special effects. Everything that is humanly possible will be used, including the excitement and the response from the audience. Michael, on many occasions, has been suspended in space. How amazing are the visual effects of lights, bombs, and fireworks!

One thing is apparent, that the performer has become one, along with thousands of people in the audience, for the period of that performance. Nothing, absolutely nothing, exists between the persona of Michael and the audience. Both the giver and the receiver are bonded together for the length of the performance and, perhaps, longer, as we shall discover later.

Each song keeps building toward the last number of the evening, both for the performer and the audience. If we were to take our eyes off of Michael for just a second, and look around at the audience, we would see some of them screaming, waving, crying, and even in rare instances, fainting. What is causing that kind of reaction? Was it the art, the notoriety, the fame, or the fantasy of the spectacle of the entertainment? Were these people expressing an act of love toward their idol?

Whatever it is, Michael is exerting an enormous influence over countless lives. While he may be leading to a climax in ending his performance, the audience is experiencing an anti-climax. In a period of approximately two hours, it's all over, and the ride home is in direct contrast to the performance. It's rather quiet and pensive as we try to grasp the significance of that very special evening and a live encounter with the megastar.

"You ask that the house lights come on and you can see their faces and say, 'Hold hands' and they hold hands and you say, 'Stand up' or 'Clap' and they do. They're enjoying themselves, and they'll do whatever you tell them. They love it and it's so beautiful -- all the races of people are together doing this. At times like that I say, 'Look around you. Look at yourselves. Look. Look around you. Look at what you have done.' Oh, it's so beautiful. Very powerful."[22]

The true significance of the concert will depend on how much thought we're willing to give the occasion. The influence of the evening will be determined in a direct ratio to the kind and amount of thought one wishes to give it, and how much one is going to value the experience. To some people, it may simply be the attainment of a dream. It might be the enjoyment and the artistry. To others, it may change the rest of their lives.

"Ever since I was a little boy, I had dreamed of creating the biggest selling record of all time. I remember going swimming as a child and making a wish before I jumped into the pool. I wanted to do something special. I'd stretch my arms out as if I were sending my thoughts right up into space. I'd make my wish, then I'd dive into the water. I'd say to myself, 'This is my dream; this is my wish'. I believe in wishes and in a person's ability to make a wish come true. I really do."[23]

Every artist expresses himself through his talent, whether it be a song, a painting, a craft, a writing; and it usually conveys a predominant theme. Once when Michael was young and being interviewed, he remarked,

"I don't sing it if I don't mean it."

Michael gives a lot of advice through the medium of song and dance. He sings about relationships between the sexes; he sings about broken relationships, and violence. He sings on issues that he feels are contemporary, and he sings about how we can improve our inner selves. Michael's theme is about beauty, caring and healing. This master definitely speaks through his music.

Through Michael's concerts, we are able to discover the traits that lead to his success. We mentioned that Michael is truly a perfectionist in all of his manifestations of his life. The attainment of perfection isn't displayed simply in the final stage of the presentation, but it is ever working, culminating to reach the goal.

The master is consistent in all of his endeavors, which is necessary to attain the desired results. At the time of seeing Michael's concerts, we are viewing the culmination of thirty-three years of training. In talking about an athlete, Michael shares the same feelings from the perspective of a performer:

> "But I identify with that person because I know how hard he trained and I know how much that moment means to him. Perhaps a whole life has been devoted to this endeavor, this one moment. And then he wins. That's the realization of a dream. That's powerful stuff. I can share that feeling because I know."[24]
> "I believe performers should be strong as an example to their audiences. It's staggering what a person can do if they only try. If you're under pressure, play off that pressure and use it to your advantage to make whatever you're doing better."[25]

We see the advancement, not only of the performer, but in technology and music. We also see the teamwork of hundreds of employees who share the same philosophy of perfection and dedication to the audience. In the *Dangerous* short film there is a portion which gives the viewer a glimpse of what it takes to set up for a presentation. The segment tells the viewer that it takes two 747 jet airplanes to transport the equipment, which includes the latest in technological equipment consisting of one hundred five lights and one hundred seventy-two speakers, with twenty-four thousand watts of power.

Upon arriving, all of this material has to be set up and in perfect operating condition. To do this efficiently requires a staff of two hundred and thirty-five people. This is what it takes at the location where the performance is being presented. It is the end result of months of planning before those huge jets even leave the ground.

The author has never been in the entertainment industry. This might be one of the reasons why she has so much admiration for the performer. The talent, the effects, and the music always have her in awe. How are they able to do so much, so elaborately, and transport it to a specific location for people to view for a few hours? With the length of scheduled performances, everything has to be dismantled and transported once again to a new location. This is done to give the spectators a good show and, no doubt, to thank them for their loyalty by lending their support to the star. After all, they have helped the star attain his success by acknowledging his talent.

To the author, there is another equally important reason. From her experience of attending a concert, the main question is, "What am I going to see, hear, and learn from the encounter?" First of all, most people go to a concert to be entertained and to have an enjoyable type of recreation. Spectators usually realize this expectation, and have a very good time.

Months and months of preparation and planning on the part of the performer are consolidated into a short space of time. While the performer is questioning and determining what he can give to his audience, the fans are anticipating what they are going to see and hear. In exhibiting his talent, he is sharing with the audience some valuable traits and what is important to him. He also reveals his philosophy in the selection of music, lyrics and dance. One could say that the performer sometimes uses selections, arrangements, or subject material from sources other than his own life experiences. However, they still state a message that the artist wants to convey and share with his audience.

"It always surprises me when people assume that something an artist has created is based on a true experience or reflects his or her own lifestyle. Often, nothing can be further from the truth. I know that I draw on my experiences at times, but I also hear and read things that trigger an idea for a song. An artist's imagination is his greatest tool. It can create a mood or feeling that people want to have, as well as transport you to a different place altogether."[26]

A master looks at life as the total sum of his experiences. An artist looks at his talent as a means of combining all of his attributes, and manifests it in a meaningful way. All the talent of this person's life is going to be exhibited in a single performance. This is another awesome concept. Here, Michael's traits of experience, training, commitment, perfectionism, and professionalism all come into play.

How does one individual execute such a feat? It starts with an idea. Next, it includes teamwork and networking. It demands paying attention to the minutest details, including timing. If the show is going to have visual effects, they have to arrive undamaged and on time. If the show is going to have other people participating, they too have to arrive at the designated time, safely and in good spirits for the task at hand.

One of the most important elements for a true master is to have the element of trust. One person's success is dependent upon many people other than himself. In direct ratio, many people's success is dependent upon one man. A master realizes both his strength and his vulnerability. A master also knows the importance of trust; both in himself and in his choice of associates.

In Michael, there are the components of strength, compassion, and sensitivity. A master knows the time, place and reason for using the elements at his disposal. While Michael's physical appearance doesn't depict a large frame, his internal strength is of giant proportions. On occasions, Michael has been called fragile. The use of adjectives in describing a person whom we do not know intimately can be incorrect and misleading. Appearances don't tell the whole story, or nor do they give an accurate picture.

Photo Courtesy of MJJ Productions

Chapter 3:

Michael Develops His Talent

"In the end, the most important thing is to be true to yourself and those you love, and to work really hard."
- Michael Jackson

A master understands that one of the most important components of his being is to establish trust. This must be done in the same proportion that the universe showers trust on its inhabitants. The world operates solely on this element, and it is exhibited with all of its manifestations: both individually, and in direct relationship, each creation with another.

If we want to fully understand how the principles of nature operate, we have to do two things: (1) Observe how the elements manifest and work together to meet a specific goal, and (2) Understand how we benefit from, interpret, and use what is provided for us.

We trust that what the universe is providing for us is always going to be present. In fact, we trust so much that we don't even give it a thought. Upon waking in the morning, we know the elements are going to be there and in proper form. We don't even take time to realize the wonderness of the universe that is responsible for holding many solar systems in place.

We have the trust in knowing that they are not going to bombard into our planet. Such natural wonders of light, air, water and gravity aren't even considered. They have been there all of our earthly life, and we trust that they will be there for our duration on the planet. Why should we doubt it?

The earth is a wonderful and beautiful teacher, providing we are in tune with the beauty of those teachings. In order to get the true understanding of nature's system of operation, one only has to look at a tree. The tree doesn't comprehend how it came to exist. It doesn't have the innate ability to realize that it came from a seed and needs nourishment. It probably doesn't realize anything at all, but it does what it has to do in order to survive. It develops a root system and becomes firmly established. Next, it commences a life long task, that of growing upward. It never looks back but keeps reaching for a specific invisible spot. As it is doing this, it nourishes both itself and the source in which it originated.

A master realizes his talent. It is something that he knows he must use and share. He knows that he must nurture his talent, and give back to the planet in the same manner which the planet so richly blessed him. He also knows that he must expand and develop that potential to his fullest capacity. While he may choose to learn from the past, his sights are always looking upward to the development of his offering to the planet, which he expresses to the highest degree that is humanly possible.

When asked if he knows how good he is, Michael responds by explaining that he never thinks about it. He simply opens his mouth and it comes out.

> "My pride in the rhythms, the technical advances, and the success of *Off the Wall* was offset by the jolt I got when the Grammy nominations were announced for 1979. Although *Off the Wall* had been one of the most popular records of the year, it received only one nomination: Best R & B Vocal Performance. I remember where I was when I got the news. I felt ignored by my peers and it hurt."

"I was disappointed and then I got excited thinking about that next album to come. All I could think of was the next album and what I would do with it. I wanted to be truly great."[27]

A master knows how to take disappointment and turn the experience into something positive. Michael mentioned that he thinks of himself as an instrument of nature. This is a very true and honest appraisal. An instrument is an implement and cannot function without the assistance of a higher source. It has a particular duty and it will perform the duty for which it was created. It will also work into close relationship to that source. The performance of that task will always be in a relationship; each party doing what it was intended to do; one to create and guide and the other to do the specific function that it was designed to do. Michael is living his life according to his belief of being an instrument of nature. He is also cognizant of knowing why the instrument was created and how to properly use it.

A master knows how to choose his associates. No one person is expected to be able to do everything himself or be an expert in every endeavor that needs to be accomplished in reaching a desired goal. Michael displays the ability to choose the proper people in assisting him to obtain the results he desires for each of his projects.

A master knows that there is always an equal exchange in the rendering of services. In the selection of top experts in the various specialty fields that are necessary in attaining goals, there is a reciprocal relationship between the creator of the idea and the people who offer and assist the master with their field of expertise. Due to this association, each party increases his knowledge by being willing to share his talent, knowledge and viewpoints with another. This is how advancement thrives.

When Michael has an idea for a short film, he enlists the talent of others to contribute to the whole scope of that idea. In working in close association with the master, the support team advances in their knowledge. We call it teamwork or networking.

However, while most individuals use those terms in the interaction in the physical world, it can take place in the brainstorming of ideas. In such cases, it takes place prior to the manifestation. In the close contact of networking, both the master and his assistants develop new techniques. Once a new skill is developed with proficiency, both sides grow and expand; not simply for one project because the new or advanced method becomes part of the reservoir of one another's creativity which can be applied in the same or different circumstances, thus leading to advancement of the art or technology.

This was illustrated in the short film *Dangerous*. The viewer had the opportunity to see how the crew worked in close communication with their boss, who just happened to be the top performer and megastar in the entertainment industry. It was amazing to feel, as an observer, the high level of energy from the fast action of the illustrations and dancing; yet at the same time, there was a naturalness and informal air to the film.

As a result of the working environment and interchange, a first class product was completed, a highly accomplished and professional piece of artistry. How do we manifest our talent to its best potential? Michael explains it in this manner:

> "In the end, the most important thing to be true to yourself and those you love and to work really hard. I mean work like there's no tomorrow. Train, strive. I mean, really train and cultivate your talent to the highest degree. Be the best at what you do. Get to know more about your field than anyone alive. Use the tools of your trade, if it's books or a floor to dance on a body of water to swim in. Whatever it is, it's yours. That's what I've always tried to remember."[28]

Reading, listening to albums, and attending concerts can have a definite effect on a person's life. What effect it will have depends on the person, his focus, his needs and his experience. The reasons may vary, but they fall into the following groups: (1) Entertainment; (2) Knowledge; (3) Inspiration, and (4) Escape.

The book has discussed the first three groups in relationship to the qualities of masters. The last group of reasoning has much more to do with us than the master. The master, being gifted, always shares that gift with others. What the individual does with the gift, once received, is totally up to him. He can hold it in high esteem. He can cherish it. He can study its features and apply it to its best usage. He can share the offering with others or, by not fully understanding the true significance, value it worthless, and wonder why he was given such a thing.

There aren't many people that would assess any contribution from a performer as worthless. However, we don't give performers the respect and honor that they deserve, and we don't keep the scale in balance with their talent and contributions to us. The scale becomes unbalanced when we attempt to incorporate actions of a personal nature into their public lives.

A master presents his message to the public on subjects and information which he deems knowledgeable, timely, or of general interest. This is the side of the personality which he naturally presents to the audience. When a person is receiving knowledge, the value or worth of such information is dependent upon the reliability of the source of which it originated.

One of the primary reasons for wanting to know about the personal lives of people in celebrity status is our curiosity; this can help us escape the rigors of daily living. It is wonderful to take time from a busy and stressful world by devoting some time to recreation or pleasure. It allows us to escape from the normal trials of living; it revitalizes us. It can take us to another time and place. It can inspire us to go for our dreams or to look at life differently, or simply let us have a passive and peaceful moment in time. It can even light a spark within our being to excel and give our lives deeper meaning.

Another reason many people like to know about the personal lives of the celebrities is to see if the presentation is consistent with their public lives. However, this can be very misleading. A rock star personality may choose to live a very quiet and peaceful life at home, and his personal taste in music may vary from his theatrical image. Knowing and exploring a celebrity's personal life serves little purpose in relationship to discovering the essence of his talent. The personal life of an individual should be private and separate from his public life, with the exception of the factors he willingly shares with other members of society.

We like to honor the contributions of entertainers. We welcome them into our hearts and homes via television, radio and stereo. We are eager to share in their success and equally saddened when adversity befalls them.

However, we have to know where to draw the line. Gossip invades the inner core of one's being and it serves no purpose in the real world of harmony and expansion. Many people not only look to entertainers for recreation, or at them out of curiosity, but as idols. They seek to compare their own lives to those of these idols.

If the entertainers show traits or a lifestyle which reflect characteristics the public determines are less than an arbitrary standard, then we say, "See, they're not so good after all." In believing this, it somehow makes our own lives more acceptable. In fact, it may make us feel that in some way, we are better than the idol and may think or respond, "Isn't that terrible? I would never do anything like that!"

This type of judgment shortens the gap of attainment between the star and the populace. People who think in this manner are forgetting a trait that everyone shares in common, and that is our human nature. No person that traverses the earth is perfect, which is the primary reason we are here; to grow, develop and expand. Mistakes are a quick learning device.

One source of information we should be careful in using regarding entertainers is the media. In times past, its purpose was to be used to report events in objective journalistic style; free from opinions or use of adjectives distorting the truth. Opinionated styles were saved for editorials. It isn't that way anymore in many cases of reporting.

Photo Courtesy of MJJ Productions

In the television special on February 10, 1993, Michael stated that he can't understand why people read the tabloids and he requested his audience not to do so. In true master style, he was a man of few words, but those words were full of meaning.

Michael understands that the media is a business and like any business, its purpose is to make money. In order to make money, it has to create and maintain a market. If there is no market, there is no business. The success of today's journalism is representative of the mentality of our minds.

If we, as a society, elevate our thinking, the media will have to change their reporting to conform to our interests. We should be interested in learning of the positive attributes of the stars. What are the contributing factors of their success? We should want news of their progress, and inspiration.

A master's words are timeless. What Michael mentioned in his book *Moonwalk* is still an appropriate evaluation of reporting today, probably even more so than when it was written. He explains in detail his opinion of the press, as he talks about the press's opinion of the quality of his speaking voice:

"Imagine the hurt of having untruths spread by the press, of having people wonder if you're telling the truth -- defending yourself because someone decided it would make good copy and would force you to deny what they said, thus creating another story. I've tried not to answer such ridiculous charges in the past because that dignifies them and the people who make them. Remember, the press is a business to make money -- sometimes at the expense of accuracy, fairness, and even the truth."[29]

Chapter 4:

Healing a Wounded World

"If you want to make the world a better place,
take a look at yourself and make a change."
~ Michael Jackson

On the cover of Michael Jackson's hit single, *Heal the World,* there is a picture of the earth with a bandaid. This is a profound and realistic symbolization depicting our wounded world because, instead of getting at the cause of our wound, we are covering up its origin.

"I am a person of the present and I have to ask, how are things going now? What's happening now? What's going to happen in the future that could affect what has happened in the past?"[30]

One of the primary reasons the issues keep perpetuating is that we are focusing on the manifestation of the wound and not on the internal cause. We seem to believe that by correcting the physical appearance, the underlying reasons will correct themselves. In other words, we are working backward. The solution is to work from the source of the problem.

Michael instructs where all of us can start to make changes in his song, *Man in the Mirror:*

"If you want to make the world a better place, Take a look at yourself and make a change."[31]

It was mentioned earlier that the home should be considered sacred. Our homes are where we are given the opportunity to be our natural and real selves. It is also the place that we establish our roots before we branch to the outside world.

A master chooses a cause, other than his craft, to which he devotes his time and effort for the betterment of mankind. For his contribution, Michael has taken on the welfare of the children of the world. He believes that children are pure, innocent, and free of judgment in their concept of the world in which they live. He also has expressed that it pains him when he sees any child suffer.

A master puts his money on his cause. Michael has established the "Heal the World Foundation." We have noted that he has terminally ill children visit and avail themselves of all the activities at his ranch. He gives large donations to charities and to individual children and their families. He even schedules visits to children in hospitals.

We know that the future of the planet lies in the hands of our children. Adults must teach our children by example. We have to display our love by giving them the security and value that they are deserving. We have to use sensitivity and caring in our nurturing, and a willingness to listen to their concerns; not just hear, but truly listen.

We have to educate our children. We need to realize that education is an ongoing process, and is universal in its scope. We have to learn not to be embarrassed when we discuss delicate subjects with our children. We shouldn't wait to start such discussions until they are already commencing adult activities.

The single bandaid covers a multitude of issues. How do we start correcting them with the quality of a master? We can learn by listening to our own self talk and paying close attention to where we secure our information. We can change, develop, and expand our thoughts just like the masters develop their talent.

Photo Courtesy of MJJ Productions

The master knows the proper use of projection, and how to avoid its misuse. He understands that projection is a valuable tool in establishing our goals, creating, or following a system in obtaining a desired result. He can also see its danger when it is misused. The master realizes that human behavior is not always consistent and is left open to the choice of the individual. Therefore, attempting to figure out another person's behavior through projection is not always reliable.

A master knows when to speak and when to remain silent. He knows that silence can be more convincing and send a message more powerful than speaking. Michael was asked why he didn't give an interview in fourteen years. He replied that he didn't feel that he had anything worthwhile to say. This doesn't infer that he didn't do anything or wasn't busy; it just means that he didn't grant any interviews. It's simple when we don't use projection.

A master treats every life experience as a learning tool and uses it to his best advantage in the development of his personal growth. People in the entertainment industry are in the limelight. We can learn from the manner of their performances a great deal about a performer's philosophy. Michael has revealed a great deal about himself; probably much more than the average performer.

In the relationship between the master and his audience, both sides have to do their part. This book has mentioned the association between the performer and audience at concerts. There is also another commitment: We know that the master always gives his best to the world, but what is the best that we can do, in turn, for the performer to maintain an equal balance in the relationship?

The best action we can take is to receive the best that the master has given. We can hold it close to our hearts and work in earnest to emulate to the world the gifts that he has given to us. This is easy when things are going along harmoniously, but what should we do if they aren't? We should be supportive in our thoughts by knowing the difference from what "could be" to "what is", and by not projecting. If we trust the wisdom of the master, we have no reason to doubt or change our minds, unless there is proof to the contrary.

We hold firm to the right of the master to keep all personal matters of his life secret. We rejoice and accept any information that he is willing to share with us by giving examples which enhance the world and ourselves.

In true master style, Michael makes excellent choices in relation to his talent, business and associates. All of his ventures carry the same attributes of the master, and all of them should be commended for the display of their own qualities of mastership.

Yes, Michael has it all -- fame, career, lifestyle, riches, investments, and enough money to grant any of his desires for the rest of his life. Yet he has one more wish that is dependent on us: That is to "simply be loved and appreciated for his talent."[32]

Michael's desire to receive love is a very basic concept. The master realizes that receiving love is necessary to receive the provisions from the planet. It is in harmony with the giver and receiver concept.

The meaning of love has been described by most artistic forms. While love has been the primary source of relationships, there are many diverse definitions. However, in giving any definition, there must be respect. This is revealed by showing acceptance and appreciation.

The master is aware of the spiritual and physical manifestations. If we don't accept ourselves for who we are, we cannot in all honesty love ourselves. By not being able to truly love our own being and therefore not experiencing the feelings, it is extremely difficult, if not impossible, to know how to accept the goodness of the planet, and see that same goodness in our fellow man.

The universe is most willing to shower its members with all necessities and the beauty of its creation. When we are able to accept all the elements that nature bestows upon us and use them to our gain, we can easily accept one another; for all of us are part of the creation.

When we accept a gift, we use what we need and share with our neighbor. This is adding to our own growth, development, knowledge, and well being. At the same time, it is helping others to do likewise. This is the highest form of a solid, healthy relationship between one another and our surroundings.

Let's see how this relationship works with Michael sharing his talent with us and, in turn, how we share it with one another and the universe. Millions of fans accept Michael's talent, which is exhibited by the staggering number of people who attend his concerts and purchase his music. We also share our feelings and emotions with him and our friends by our actions. Many people belong to his fan clubs and spend endless hours listening and discussing his music and short films with one another.

While Michael wants to be loved and appreciated for his music, he also wants to be simply loved. If we use the components of appreciation and acceptance as our criteria, the former goes without question. A master takes the whole scope of a belief and then breaks it down to specifics. He realizes that the minute particles all carry the attributes of the whole.

In interpersonal relationships, if you accept a part of an individual's characteristics, you are accepting the entire person. You may not agree with some facets of that person, but you cannot take only a portion of a person. If you accept Michael's talent, you accept Michael, because Michael is his talent and his talent is him. His creativity in the layout of his ranch, his recreation, his business, and the like, are all an integral part of his whole person.

Of all the definitions associated with love, acceptance is one of the primary elements. Nothing brings this fact to light more vividly than in our association with children. We have mentioned the importance of having good self-esteem and how it assists in giving empowerment to the individual. Children must be accepted for who they are, and not what we may want them to be.

This is not to undermine good discipline and training. It means that we cannot have some preconceived idea of what we want them to be. This is one of the quickest ways to stifle creativity. Love is unconditional acceptance.

A master is in tune with the inner core of his being. In studying Michael Jackson, this is his highest attribute. While the world applauds the accomplishments, the author applauds the man. She is honored to live in the same era of a man of his caliber. One does not do anything worthwhile without receiving personal benefits.

Michael lives his life according to his terms. He exhibits two of the most essential absolutes of life by his lifestyle: (1) Live a life that experiences the gifts of the Creator, individually and jointly, by using your talents for the betterment of mankind and the planet; and (2) Always be true to yourself.

We live in a country that offers each person so much. We have the modern conveniences that make our lives easy. We have the choice of obtaining anything that we desire, thus giving us the opportunity to fulfill any of our dreams and aspirations. Michael, by his example, is one of the masters who has taught us how to prosper and to protect the source that has given us these provisions.

As with everything else in life, all we have to do is to look within ourselves for the correct solution. When we take ammunition and use that material to tell the other country we are serious and by the use of our force and might, they better conform, we must first ask ourselves what the outcome of such a decision encompasses in its entirety.

First, we must recall that the master never uses force as the means to unite another person into his thought process. He uses his creative source. He focuses on the problems. He uses himself as an example, and he does all this with love. This love permeates every component that is an integral part of the whole situation. To really understand the working of the master, let's explore each of the attributes of the components of his thought process and apply it to our present method of solving world problems.

In the use of this creative process, the master looks at the present method of what has been manifested. He studies the result. He asks himself if he can contribute to the existing experience or create a better or more innovative way by understanding the end result that he is attempting to attain. He may decide to modify, revise, or expand an idea or solution by expansion and taking it to a higher level. This is how advancement takes place.

In using himself as an example, and while he has to portray the proper behavior, the master has to extend that example in the form of the feelings that the populace is going to experience as the result of the use of his intuition. He receives a visual picture of both the present actions and wha the new contribution will achieve.

When Michael Jackson starts with a new idea for a song or dance, he must project in his mind how his fans or audience are going to respond to his offering, and if it will be the response that he desires from them. This is what a master always does. He searches for the very best response for what he is attempting to accomplish. If the results are in direct conflict to the purpose, he modifies them or uses an entirely different approach that draws on a contrasting method or is innovative by the creative process. The same method is the positive approach in discovering the solutions to contemporary issues of our generation.

One of the most important concerns for the twentieth century is our ability to get along and to work for the better advancement of the planet. How do we do this? Yes, we have to project the feelings that we would experience if we are going to use the solutions we envisioned for another individual.

Most of the inhabitants of the planet are average citizens of a country. We want peace and harmony. This is dependent upon the people who serve in leadership capacities. In our country, they are elected or appointed. These government officials' prime duty is to ensure that we are able to enact our regular activities while we are residing on the planet.

What would happen if any nation decided to inflict nuclear war on another opposing country? A master could easily envision the results. The problem originated with the select leadership of the country and not the citizens. Yet thousands of innocent people will lose the gift of their life.

If you use yourself as an example, one knows the results. You could be at work. You could be walking in the street. You could be anywhere and you hear an announcement to run for cover. You may be one of the lucky ones to survive but you may have suffered a great loss as some members of your family and friends may not have been so fortunate.

This, of course, is oversimplified. The most horrendous effect of nuclear war is that it would infiltrate the minutest particles of life and civilization. The very thing that we desire most is insuring a peaceful existence. The master looks at the possible results of his talent and determines if it is going to bring the results he desires from his heart. The use of such powerful means as nuclear war is not employing a peaceful means of action. How can we enjoy peace, if we may no longer be physically present to experience the very thing we are earnestly seeking?

We are not showing our thankfulness and appreciation for the provisions of the planet. We are not giving it the love and care that it rightfully deserves. We must learn from the example of the master in knowing the proper use of the blessings that have been generously provided for our welfare and happiness.

The effectiveness of any creation is evaluated by its ability to fulfill its purpose. Before the attribute of power is used, the purpose must be defined. In the case of forming a military and giving it the proper tools to perform its purpose, we most certainly have to ascertain the function of the creation and its usage. If the purpose of the armed services and the development of advanced forms of ammunition are established with the prime idea of keeping our borders free from attack, the purpose is clearly defined and would not be used for any other reason.

When we tread another nation's soil, the purpose has to be clear. If we believe that we are an advanced country who sincerely believes in the freedom of mankind, then all of our thought processes must reflect that motive. In doing so, we set a precedent policy, we are telling all the nations of the world that this is the method for solving issues. You have to forget what we say, preach, or believe, it is the action we take that tells what we think.

Michael Jackson has stated many times, and in diverse ways, that his solution to heal the world is by the act of displaying love. The people of the world love Michael Jackson. If you ask them why, they will say that he is a good person. They love his talent. They love that he lends a helping hand. They look with interest at his lifestyle. Yet, they will readily admit, they don't know how he does it and can't state what their attraction to this master is in a simple, all-inclusive answer.

People who have followed Michael's career know that he is a very soft, sensitive, and caring individual. He is always striving for perfection in all facets of life. However, while we see his solution as being in perfect harmony to his beliefs, we also see it as sweet and caring, and perhaps rather simplistic. Therefore, we tend to overlook its power.

The declaration is so powerful that if it was applied properly to any interaction we have with another individual, there would be no conflict. The reason is that if you desire to use the components of true love -- respect, acceptance, and appreciation -- you would hold the value of life in such esteem that the empowerment for peaceful means would be dominant within you and flow outward in the physical environment. It has nothing to do with controlling a situation but with sharing the fine attributes each has and combining them in a peaceful manner.

The formula for getting along with any other individual is done through the enactment of love. In displaying love, criticizing another is not the way of obtaining conformity. If you truly love another, you help bring out their highest qualities by the education and training that you exhibit and are willing to share with one another.

To criticize, to judge, to project an arbitrary code of behavior is wrong. It is not creating the type of relationship all of us should share with one another. If we want to have a balanced existence, all of us have to embrace one another, and sometimes even carry one another until the wounds of the other person are healed. When a brother, sister, or country is in need, we should willingly come to their aid and give them the shelter of our own hearts. To find our own success, happiness, or self worth by exploiting their misfortune is, in essence, acting out our own insecurities and mirroring our own behavior.

Masters live an extremely vulnerable life. They are visible before the mass population. While we see their success, we also become keenly aware of their short comings. The public can be quite fickle. We can put an entertainer on a pedestal, and then let him plummet just as quickly. Due to this exposure, an entertainer can be famous one season and a has-been the next.

Michael Jackson has maintained his reputation, popularity, and standard of excellence for thirty-three years. He has become a legend, oblivious to time.

"The price of fame can be a heavy one. Is the price you pay worth it? Consider that you really have no privacy. I've been accused of being obsessed with my privacy and it's true, I am. People stare at you when you are famous. They're always observing you and that's understandable, but it's not always easy."[33]

Elizabeth Taylor's statement of Michael Jackson being "larger than life" is a true description and an accurate one, if you are taking into consideration his accomplishments. The deciding factor, however, transcends the material manifestations. One has to realize that this person's thought process is the asset that puts him in the stature of being an American Master for the last decade of the twentieth century.

People all over the world revere his dedication and effort in making "the world a better place", but most of all, we revere his belief that it can be done. This undertaking means that all people are going to have to join in the calling and unite with a common purpose.

"It's been my dream since I was a child to somehow unite people all over the world through love and music." [34]

After all, in the end, that's what it is all about. It's not about putting people in separate categories. It's about oneness. It's breaking down barriers. It's about taking on responsibility for our own actions. It's about acceptance and not judgments. It's looking within and using the creative source to establish new solutions to old problems. Most of all, it's taking our clue and example from the masters!

The Master's Latest Message
"The Dream Continues..."

In the middle of 1995, Michael Jackson began to send out new messages. The public marked the calendar for June 14 and 15. His new short film, *Scream*, was premiered, and the next evening his first live interview since January, 1993, was aired. Prior to these two events, his *HIStory* trailer was flashed across the screen in movie theaters and on television for weeks.

After viewing these presentations, the populace went into a fury, expressing their opinions in the press, on the radio and on television. Did these three forms of the media give an unbiased, comprehensive, and accurate account of Michael Jackson's message? What you seek is what you will find.

There are always consistency and continuity in the messages of the master. In the trailer, we see thousands of troops in Budapest, Hungary, marching on two sides of Michael, coming down the center of the aisle. He is radiant, and waves to the crowds who are in awe with the new leader who is displaying his devotion by the smile on his face.

The scene changes to a foundry where workers are creating a statue. You can see the perspiration pouring from their bodies as they toil in the heat from the furnaces. The film flashes to the city square, where the citizens are running. There are helicopters overhead, and a man preparing to remove the cover on the statue. Another man adjusts his safety glasses, ready to reveal the monument of the new leader.

Then, unveiled, we see a statue of Michael Jackson, while fireworks explode in the background. A young boy looks with wonderment at the new vision before his eyes, and expresses his love for Michael. The helicopters fly above and under the statue. Here is Michael, in all of his glory, portrayed by the height and presence of a monumental work of steel.

On Wednesday evening, June 15, 1995, at ten o'clock, sixty million people tuned their television in to hear and view Michael Jackson's interview with Diane Sawyer on *PrimeTime Live*. The presentation was comprehensive, offering the populace a glimpse into the new life experiences of Michael Jackson, as well as showing *Scream* and discussing the *HIStory* trailer as an introduction to his new two-disc CD. This new package, titled *HIStory, Past, Present and Future Book 1*, includes thirty songs and was released on June 20, 1995. Fifteen of the songs are new releases, and fifteen are hit songs from throughout the years.

A master is always consistent in his beliefs and in his demeanor with the public. There have been many changes in Michael's life since his 1993 interview with Oprah Winfrey, but there are many similarities in the manner in which he responded to the probing questions from Diane Sawyer. The inquiries were in two distinct areas: (1) The personal life of the couple; and (2) The new manifestations of the master.

During the past two years, the general public hasn't changed its focus on the type of information it desires to learn from celebrities, and the new family was not an exception. The message of the book explains to the reader that information on the personal life of a celebrity serves little purpose in understanding the talent or thought process depicted in the celebrity's craft.

During the first part of the interview, Michael expressed that he didn't care to live in America, and hopes, in fact, to live in another country such as Switzerland or South Africa. He said that he cannot tolerate the smog of Los Angeles, but that he will always keep his Neverland Valley Ranch. This should give Americans some comfort in knowing that he will maintain a residence within our borders.

Many Americans would be saddened to see Michael move to take up permanent residence in another country. However, again, people have to look within themselves. If they want celebrities to continue to live in our country, it is necessary to give them the honor and respect of which they are most deserving. The citizens have to explore their own thought process, and decide if they have given Michael the proper respect he deserves. It is inhuman to think that the media, and some of the public, can form opinions through the use of projection, which is not based on truth, and then expect masters to continue to feel comfortable in the confines of our country. Here, we have to determine if it's the smog of the universe or the "smog" in our own manner of gathering and accepting information. Cleaning up the atmosphere is an easy task compared to changing the way we form judgments.

The second part of the PrimeTime interview premiered Michael's first short film, *Scream*, from his new CD. *Scream* opened on the Billboard charts at number five that very night. Within a few weeks, he released two more short films, *Childhood* and *You Are Not Alone*. In the next few years, we will view additional short films to accompany other songs on this CD.

The short film *Scream* is a futuristic illustration of the lyrics to the song by the same name. It commences with a space ship flying through the universe. Inside the ship, the viewer is shown a panel where the travelers can obtain stress capsules. Michael and his sister, Janet Jackson, can be seen in pain, holding their hands on the side of their faces, screaming. The caricature on the big screen is also shown screaming. The main rooms of the ship include a gallery, meditation and recreation room. Conditions flash on the screen, such as GRAVity, MEDitation, and reCREATion. Since the ship is free of gravity, the travelers are free to climb the walls and ceiling.

There is interpretive dancing which shows anger, confusion, and frustration. Michael and Janet play a computer game together. We see Michael destroying artifacts, and the glass cover in the meditation room shatters. The travelers receive news from a commentator on Earth. While Michael receives a direct message from Earth, Janet goes into a room, and in total aggravation, sends out a message.

Of course, during these different illustrations, Janet and Michael are singing the lyrics to the song. They describe Michael's understanding of the issues of his generation. In true mastership form, he uses himself to express his interpretation of our plight through the words:

Scream

"Tired of injustice
Tired of the schemes
Kinda disgusted
So what does it mean
Kicking me down
I got to get up
As jacked as it sounds
The whole system sucks"

"Peek in the shadow
Come into the light
You tell me I'm wrong
Then you better prove you're right
You're selling out souls but
I care about mine
I've got to get stronger
And I won't give up the fight"

"With such confusion don't it make you wanna scream
Your bash abusin' victimize within the scheme"

"You try to cope with every lie
they scrutinize
Somebody please have mercy
'cause I just can't take it
Stop pressurin' me
Just stop pressurin' me..."

"Tired of you tellin' the story your way
It's causing confusion
You think it's okay"

"Keep changing the rules
While you're playing the game
I can't take it much longer
I think I might go insane..."

"You find your pleasure scandalizin' every lie

Oh father, please have mercy 'cause
I just can't take it
Stop pressurin' me
Just stop pressurin' me..."
"Oh my God, can't believe what I saw
As I turned on the TV this evening
I was disgusted by all the injustice
All the injustice"

"A man has been brutally beaten
to death by Police after being wrongly
identified as a robbery suspect.
The man was an 18 year old black male..."
(repeats and chorus)[35]

The song *Childhood* is the theme song for the new motion picture, *Free Willy 2*. In the accompanying short film, the diversity of Michael's creativity becomes apparent. While the short film, *Scream*, advances the viewer into the future by expressing issues that are presently confronting our planet in the form of making judgments, *Childhood* takes the audience into the past where Michael sees the perfect, dreamy, uninhibited world of children.

While the atmosphere of *Scream* shows Janet and Michael traveling in the realm of outer space, *Childhood* portrays Michael sitting solidly on the ground in the beautiful habitat of a natural forest. He is pensively reminiscing the childhood that he was deprived of in lieu of pursuing his talent. *Childhood* does not exclude the serenity of the vastness of the universe. Children float in boats high above Michael in the peaceful caress of the sky. One young boy walks through the forest and looks in awe at the sight of the boats and children playing baseball high in the air. He is gently transferred from the ground up into one of the boats.

The lyrics of the master's song carry the message of trying hard to not judge Michael but to love him:

Childhood

"Have you seen my childhood?
I'm searching for the world that I come from
'Cause I've been looking around
In the lost and found of my heart...
No one understands me
They view it as such strange eccentricities
'Cause I keep kidding around
Like a child, but pardon me..."

                                        "People say I'm not okay
                                  'Cause I love such elementary things
                           It's been my fate to compensate for the childhood
                                        I've never known"

"Have you seen my Childhood?
I'm searching for that wonder in my youth
Like pirates in adventurous dreams,
Of conquest and kings on the throne"

                                              "Before you judge me
                                                try hard to love me,
                                     Look within your heart then ask,
                                     Have you seen my Childhood?"

"People say I'm strange that way
'Cause I love such elementary things,
It's been my fate to compensate
for the childhood I've never known"

                                        "Have you seen my Childhood?
                                  I'm searching for that wonder in my youth
                                        Like fantastical stories to share
                                  The dreams I would dare, watch me fly"

"Before you judge me,
try hard to love me
The painful youth I've had"

                                        "Have you seen my Childhood"[36]

The short film, *You Are Not Alone*, premiered simultaneously on three networks. Bill Bellamy of MTV hosted the half-hour special, in which he held a surprise interview with Michael Jackson. Michael discussed questions featuring the new CD. The master's presentation is consistent. Michael appeared relaxed and displayed a soft demeanor.

You Are Not Alone features Michael in an empty theater, expressing his feelings for his wife, Lisa Marie. It also features Lisa Marie for the first time in a short film. The other stage backgrounds depict natural, yet stark, scenery entirely unlike any seen in the previously released short films, Scream and *Childhood*.

This short film reveals a new side to Michael's creativity, relying on intense feelings and sensitivity to express his deep love for Lisa Marie. He depicts the physical closeness between two people who feel such a deep passion toward one another, and at the same time transcends physical love.

A master understands sharing the benefits of his talent. Michael Jackson has, once again, set up a scholarship. This time it is for little Craig Fleming's surviving brother, Michael, to ensure a future of possibilities through the development of his talent.

Michael has also been extremely busy bringing the masses much knowledge and enjoyment. All of his songs and short films convey messages which will enhance the public and advance each individual's thinking and creative processes to a higher level.

When reviewed by the masses, the lyrics to Michael's songs offer the opportunity to form judgments about the messages. It is important to remember that making judgments are subject to the mind of the individual, and are not real in the physical world. It is prudent to analyze the entire scope of the works of talented, creative people. If words are used that are stark, it is necessary to trace their origin. Society forms the distinction of words and categories. Even so, it is dangerous to take words, phrases or opinions out of the context in which they were intended to create meaning.

Music critics and journalists have given their opinion of Michael's presentations. They have attempted to determine his future and his beliefs on the condition of the world. They have attempted to find the reasoning to his illustrations and lyrics of his new CD and *HIStory* movie trailer. They ask why he uses such frank and descriptive vocabulary.

Some critics believe that the *HIStory* short film was modeled after Leni Riefenstahl's 1935 *Triumph of the Will*. Other critics believe that some of his lyrics in one of his songs were anti-Semitic. What did Michael really mean? Again, it is best to apply his advice to not judge a person unless you speak to him one on one. On *PrimeTime*, he stated that he was outraged that he was so misunderstood. He explained that the particular song they were referring to was meant to bring people's attention to social and political problems:

"I am not the one who was attacking. It is about the injustices to young people, and how the system can wrongfully accuse them."[37]

In so far as the *HIStory* trailer is concerned, Michael said,

"It has nothing to do with politics, communism, or fascism... You don't see any tanks and you don't see any cannons. It's about love, people coming together. It's art."[38]

Perhaps, Michael's manager knows his client well. When he was asked about the lyrics to *They Don't Care About Us*, Mr. Sandy Gallin said that they should be kept in context:

"When I heard those lyrics, I thought they were brilliant. He is saying stop labeling people, stop degrading people, stop calling them names."[39]

Remember that a master always uses what he does know to find the solutions to the unknown. By taking Michael's example and listening to the lyrics, we are able to discover the intent of his message.

A master also has a keen sense of timing for presenting his wisdom to the populace, and he uses himself as the prime example. In the time since Michael's last album, there have been many changes in the world. Perhaps the issues involved were always present, but they have become more of the norm in the daily lives of the inhabitants of the planet.

It is well known that Michael Jackson is an innovator of our time. In the display of his talent, he is way ahead of contemporary methods most artists use to express their craft. In *Scream*, he expresses his exasperation of injustice, especially that of opinions formed by the masses about individuals.

He advises the viewer and listener to come out of the shadows and into the light; if they are going to tell him that he is wrong, they better prove themselves right. In essence, society is selling out souls, but he won't give up the fight. In the pretend newscast, he gives an example of how quickly the police will make judgments and even cause an individual to lose the gift of life through their wrong choice. The populace is tired of the violence and the various types of abuse circulating in its midst. Yet society finds relief in using an individual to represent the wrongness of a popular or current issue.

It is important to remember that violence begets violence. A master never uses force to enlist people into his thought process. He uses his talent to send out the message that he believes is timely and of service to mankind.

When Michael decides he is going to do a project, he networks with the best people in all endeavors to bring the manifestation to the heights of perfectionism. All of his associates involved on the set of the short film, *Scream*, speak very highly of Michael Jackson, and feel extremely honored that he would engage them to assist and offer their individual talents to complete the work. It is positive to note that they expressed that he was a regular person who interacted with them.

If people really want to learn the thought process of the master, they have to exert some energy by doing a little research. By not doing so, they can be caught up in the controversy, to which Michael says, "Good, they fell into the trap."[40]

The "trap" is relying on a person's own judgment without searching and researching for the truth. A trap is a form of restraint. A person who has not searched for himself can easily find himself in the mental thought process of others who have not adequately done their homework. The way out of a trap is to search the lessons and knowledge of people who have encountered similar situations, and apply wisdom through intuition.

A master always has multiple purposes in his message. He desires to make it easy for the populace to arrive at the message of love and not judgment. Michael gives a clue in the title of his album, *HIStory, Past Present and Future, Book 1*. First, it is part of his life (his story). Second, it is the history of the past (the condition of some past governments), and the future (the use of a spaceship to break through the inconsistencies of the planet on which we reside).

The individual who really desires to understand would study the past ideology of countries that did not practice a democratic way of life. Michael then offers the student a solution; that of operating from the framework of love. One might also find it beneficial to study some of the past masters. They had to face the very same problems that Michael is experiencing, both personal and public. The past masters found it necessary to leave their home cities and exhibit their craft in another location. Michelangelo traveled to neighboring cities when there was strife in his home city of Florence. He was always interested in its government, although at times it brought him much sadness:

> "Michelangelo seems to have tried, thereby, to set a moral and physical prototype that should inspire the citizens to defend the republic and its just government. It was a novelty to represent David in this way...lacking the traditional attributes...vigilance, fortitude and anger that the Florentine humanists regarded as the greatest of civic virtues."

> "He left his seal of his personality on the principal ecclesiastical and civil monuments already in existence. He used David, the symbol of republican liberty, to be set up in order to bring out the significance of the Palazzo, itself the seat of the republican government."[41]

Michelangelo studied the other masters who had displayed their talents. He had a good memory, and while he never copied their work, he learned the techniques they applied to their craft. He advanced his art by taking it to a higher level than the other masters of his selected craft.

All of Michael Jackson's music carries a message. He is a learned man. He reads and studies anything remotely related to his particular field of expertise. By studying the entire scope of his talent, he can apply ideas and techniques of the past and present to enhance his manifestations into the future.

Michael has used every means to enhance his most recent CD and short films. The populace is entranced by the costs of such an extravaganza. Expense is not important in the mind of the master. He is most interested in breaking and surpassing his past accomplishments. It is the challenge.

Michael is most happy when he is engaging in the composition and creation of his music and performances. Seeing the fans rejoice and unite in a common experience fills his heart and soul, and nourishes his life force.

There is much for his audiences, readers and listeners, to learn. They too should fill their souls with the vibrations of this master's creativity as it is reflected in his music and dance. The public can increase their enjoyment and knowledge by sharing in his thought process and his high standard of excellence. All of America should embrace and claim this master. While he shares his talent with the world, he was born and nurtured his talent in America. Millions of children have grown up with his music, and he continues to move forward.

The population can advance along with the master if they look for the purity and innocence of life. True acceptance comes through the act of love in cherishing our own gift of time on the planet. We do not own any property, claim any possession of another authority, nor have as our purpose to judge or condemn any of nature's creation. We are guests of the planet, directed to share its wonders.

The lyrics of *Scream* reveal that it is prudent to exercise compassion toward our fellow man. By not doing so, we can make a man such as Michael, with his soft manner and sensitivity toward the provisions of the planet, want to Scream.

One of the profound characteristics of the masters is that they take their talent to the next plane of beauty and understanding. Their principles are timeless. The plot of *Scream* will be of interest for people of many generations to come. In future decades, the spaceship may become a normal mode of traveling.

The message is universal, and timeless too. The master knows that thoughts are electrical impulses and that they advance through the invisible realm of the atmosphere. The lesson in *Scream* may be that until man can live peacefully on earth and forego judgments, the thought process which we apply on the planet will follow us wherever we may go.

There was a hush all over the world on the night of September 7, 1995, as the multitude of viewers were glued to their television sets to see the annual MTV Video Music Awards broadcast from Radio City Music Hall in New York City. The media interviewed the cream of the crop in music entertainment prior to the presentation. Many of the artists spoke of their anticipation and excitement at the opportunity to, once again, see the megastar of the entertainment industry perform live before their very eyes.

The admiration was well warranted, and the world was not disappointed. Michael opened the Awards with a fourteen minute rendition of a medley of his greatest hits, and then a song from his new *HIStory* album.

Michael has a deep and sincere love for all mankind. The master fully understands the reciprocal relationship of love between the giver and the receiver. Thus, simply, his presence was all it took to generate a high level of energy throughout the auditorium. It was apparent that the admiration from the audience was genuine. They started to proclaim their love by the clapping, waving, and cheering before Michael even sang his first note.

Photo Courtesy of MJJ Productions

A master is always consistent in revealing his essence and talent, and always gives his very best in interacting with his audience. The performance showed Michael's dedication to his craft, and he was in top form. It was typical of his standard of always attaining perfection, and representative of the high level of creativity and execution of talent of a master. In keeping with the presentation of a master, Michael also acknowledged his appreciation for the artistry of Slash, who has been featured before as one of Michael's lead guitarists.

The choreography and setting were perfect. Michael's movements were sharp and direct, and his footwork characteristically smooth. In anticipating the wishes of his audience, Michael included such favorites as *Billy Jean*, *Dangerous*, and *Smooth Criminal*.

You Are Not Alone, a Number One hit from *HIStory*, was the final selection of Michael's presentation, and he took the stage solo. At the end of the song, the camera panned to his sister, Janet, an artist in her own right. She was looking at her brother with pride and awe at his performance. Her response was representative of the entire audience's respect and admiration for the top performer in the entertainment industry. Of course, Michael's radiant and sincere smile was infectious.

It was truly a special evening. In reporting the event, newspapers around the world headlined Michael for having received not just one, but three awards. Michael and Janet were each awarded for their artistry in the Best Dance Video. A master always respects and acknowledges his love for his family, and it was easy to discern the love that both of them have for each other. These same feelings were shared by everyone, including the millions of viewers around the world who were fortunate to witness the presentation in their homes.

In reading through the various chapters and pages of this book, one can experience the deep emotion, love and concern that Michael Jackson shares with the planet and the various inhabitants which make this globe their home. Each creature has the pleasure of enjoying one of the universe's celestial bodies as their home on which to grow and expand. With such an awesome gift comes grave responsibility to maintain order, and protect and enhance the planet. The master illustrates this understanding in his outward manifestations. This can only be developed through his thought process. Unless each individual bases his thought process on knowledge and application of universal principles, both man and the planet could be in jeopardy.

Michael brought forth this concept en force through the releases of his newest short films. *Scream* informs the viewer, as he looks into the future, what happens if his thought process doesn't keep up with modern technology. Man will face the same issues no matter how he attempts to escape.

In the short film, *Childhood*, the words of the song remind the viewer how the early years of development can have a profound effect on the adult years. Michael reminds the populace not to judge his life experiences. In fact, such encounters helped to mold and enhance his offerings to the world.

While *You Are Not Alone* is illustrated as a beautiful love song between husband and wife, it reveals universal concepts. It explains that although one may not be physically present, individuals can communicate through the invisible portion of space and time. Such communication is real; distance does not need to hinder the true presence of individuals.

In the summer of 1995, Michael was asked on Internet what his favorite song on his new album is. He replied that it is *Earth Song.* In November, 1995, Michael presented his fourth short film from *HIStory. Earth Song* was debuted on three major entertainment channels. Upon seeing the short film, it is not difficult to see that value of his response on Internet.

Scream and *Childhood* appeal to the thought process of each individual and are based on personal experiences of the master, as is *You Are Not Alone. Earth Song* unites all of mankind to take a very serious look at our present thought process; are we culminating to destroy all stages of life?

He gives the populace a profound picture of what man's actions and solutions have done to the planet. The short film shows, through Michael's eyes, the intense feelings of anguish and despair he is experiencing as he views the condition of the planet as a result of man's selfishness. Tractors, saws and fire destroy our precious forests; war ravages families and children; industrial pollution destroys our air; and man's greed results in the senseless killing of innocent animals.

In this short film, the master isn't the only individual who can't escape the results of disaster. Families appear with disbelief at the carelessness and selfishness of man's short-sighted remedies to an already troubled world. Along with Michael, they humble themselves, falling to their knees and clutching the earth in their hands in despair. The Earth begins to scream, and the winds force them to brace themselves, hanging on for life.

Michael, braced between two trees left in the forest, cries out. As Michael sings these lyrics, the Creator responds to his plea. The earth is being restored to its natural state, as the winds spin the planet in reverse. The people witness the trees returned upright in all their natural beauty; the elephant's husks are restored to the dead carcass, and it regains its life. Dolphins swim freely, the greenery of the soil reappears, and armies are forced back. A man shot in the back awakens, stands up and faces the force of the wind.

When man's requests come from the outpouring of the soul, and not his rational mind, his pleas are always answered by the Creator, who wants the spirituality of His manifestations to be in harmony with the master plan of His universe.

Earth Song

"..Hey, what about yesterday
What about the seas
The heavens are falling down
I can't even breathe
What about the bleeding Earth
Can't we feel its wounds
What about nature's worth
It's our planet's womb
What about animals
We've turned kingdoms to dust
What about elephants
Have we lost their trust
What about crying whales
We're ravaging the seas
What about forest trails
Burnt despite our pleas

What about the holy land
Torn apart by creed
What about the common man
Can't we set him free
What about children dying
Can't you hear them cry
Where did we go wrong
Someone tell me why
What about babies
What about the days
What about all their joy
What about the man
What about the crying man
What about Abraham
What about death again
Do we give a damn..."[42]

When this short film was first viewed by the author, the tears flowed freely. This is a very personal side of Michael, and the Creator. It gave this viewer determination to appreciate, love and continue to nurture the planet. In this film's beauty, it touches the soul. But it is a profound warning.

In harmonizing with the desired thought process of the master, and taking the short film to the next level, it is hoped that *Earth Song* will become a new type of documentary and used on a global scale. It could be viewed in the higher institutes of learning, appearing in colleges and universities as a visual example and spurring the creativity of future scholars. It is also suggested by this author that each home have a copy to share with family members and initiate discussion.

People watching *Entertainment Tonight* on April 8, 1996, received a treat in seeing some of Michael's work on his latest short film, *They Don't Care About Us.* The short film then premiered on BET during the week.

The setting for the film is the inner city of Rio de Janeiro, Brazil. Michael had hundreds of young residents beating brightly painted drums as he sang the lyrics. The sound of the drums brings forth the intensity of the hearts of these young persons. In the short film, it is heard all around the city and countryside. In truth, the vibration of the drums bypasses the eardrums and pierces the physical image of mankind like an arrow to the soul of each viewer. It is as if the children are saying, "The drums in our music are revealing the beat of our hearts. Hear our plea...Care about us."

Like all of Michael's short films, the message is massive and powerful. At the end of the film, one young man is holding his drum and striking it with conviction. Michael is next to him, raising his hand, mimicking the same movement. The enactment of the song, *They Don't Care About Us*, reveals Michael's urgency and compelling message of the need of mankind to care about the plight of children all over the globe.

Spike Lee, the director, commented that Michael had told him it was his desire to make *They Don't Care About Us* his best short film yet. A trip to one of our neighboring countries, thousands of children dressed in white tee-shirts white tennis shoes, all beating drums, and the master singing his heart out with his message...What could be more awesome?

On December 5, 1995, the news of Michael Jackson's health was broadcast throughout the world. For those people who were tuned in to their television sets or radios, the media kept the populace informed concerning the latest medical reports on the master's condition.

Michael was rehearsing for his televised concert at the Beacon Theater in New York when he was taken seriously ill. He was transported to the hospital immediately and spent almost a week in intensive care. Instantly, newscasters attempted speculation for the sudden illness.

The public should be concerned about Michael's well being, rather than the exact medical implications and severity. For days, there were news clips and radio coverage. The media reported that he was suffering from extremely low blood pressure, dehydration and exhaustion. The exact symptoms reported varied, and so did the causes. What the mass did know, though, was that it was serious; serious enough to last for a week.

A master always strives for perfection in illustrating his craft. This requires mental, emotional and physical endurance. Sometimes, it is more than the body's resources can tolerate, and the body breaks down. This condition affects various organs of the body, and can be serious. It is a profound warning for the master to slow down and temporarily curtail his activities and strenuous schedule.

The whole world felt sorrow and compassion for Michael's medical condition, and opened up its heart with concern and an outpouring of gifts and cards. Michael appreciated such efforts, and believes that such a display expedited his recovery -- enough for him to leave the hospital. When someone who has given of himself for the betterment of mankind, the population shifts into action and exhibits their love and appreciation. It is equally important for the mass to continue to have Michael in their hearts and prayers at all times. As the master gives of himself, all of us should continue to have his health and well-being uppermost in our consciousness.

In realizing the attributes of love, the physical union of the couple, Michael Jackson and Lisa Marie Presley, dissolved on January 18, 1996. In correlating this action in accordance with universal principles, all creation, upon the completion of a manifestation, has the innate ability to know when to let go. In life, when a person truly loves another, he knows when it is beneficial to let an individual go, so that individual can advance and fulfill the purpose and destiny which is inherent within his or her being. The union of Michael Jackson and Lisa Marie Presley has become part of their personal history.

In a healthy family, the parents apply the very same universal principle in their interaction with their children. When children have gained all the insights of being immediate members of the original family, they branch out in order to conquer new horizons on their own. However, the teaching experiences and love of the family follow them throughout their adult life.

On November 14, 1996 Michael Jackson and Debbie Rowe were married during his concert tour in Australia. The previous Sunday,, Michael Jackson announced, during an exclusive interview with VH1, that the information circulating for the past week was indeed accurate. Michael Jackson and Debbie Rowe are expecting the birth of their first child in February 1997.

Once again, the master is sharing his talent with the world. Masters always share their talent for the betterment of mankind and the planet. It is a natural phenomenon for nature to manifest in equal likeness so that its beauty can perpetuate and be experienced by future generations.

The real news is that Michael has now insured that future generations will continue to have his talent through the heritage of the lifeline of his family. The child will have a panorama of opportunity to become all that he can be. Congratulations are in order for the parents-to-be, and the world as we experience the rebirth of the father through his child.

We know, after reading to this point in the book, that Michael Jackson takes the gift of his talent to the highest level possibly attainable. We have learned, too, that a master takes the essentials of his talents to the field of business. In doing this, he opens his primary artistry into the advancement of his individual goals and for the betterment of mankind.

In experiencing life, Michael knows the skills, techniques and recreational pursuits which bring him much enjoyment and pleasure, and enhance his business acumen. In March 1996, he held a press conference with the Prince of Saudia Arabia to announce their plans for a new mega-million dollar joint venture. Kingdom Entertainment includes plans for worldwide theme parks, and a new movie-production house.

This effort will bring fun and joy to many youth, and adults too, to encourage a healthy and wholesome way of spending time. It should help to spur creativity in people, as it does in Michael, by partaking in manifestations of others. It gives people the experience of excitement, thrill, and perhaps escape from the rigors of life for awhile. In being able to do this, they can dream about another phase of man's assets -- day dreaming and applying intuition. They may get the thought that, if one man can have such a dream of enhancing the world, they, too, can use their ingenuity and break the barriers of arbitrary boundaries in the world that man has created for himself.

We should recall the love that Michael is willing to give the public and his loyal fans. Michael's intent is to enhance the world through the expertise of his craft, and share his feelings on the purpose of life and the conditions, issues and plight of the planet.

In a true sense, since we have an outward picture of how much he has given, we should keep the vision of the master in our minds and rejoice in his offerings. Now we know the great sacrifice he is willing to make in order to make this world of ours a much better place. We should be exceedingly thankful for his contributions throughout his life for the Creator's children and the preservation of the planet.

The master has given the world a priceless gift. This leads to a question. As the receiver of such an awe-inspiring gift, what is the universal family going to do with this lesson and message?

Michael has done exceedingly well in the last two years. He has advanced to another plateau of accomplishment. The passing of time leads Michael to greater heights in illustrating his talent. He commenced his *HIStory* world tour on September 7, 1996, and scheduled thirty-seven concert dates through the end of December 1996. The tour, part of his joint venture with Kingdom Entertainment, is expected to last through 1998.

Yes, the dream is continuing in Michael's life and in the lives of the people of the world as they view the accomplishments of the master. He truly has made *HIStory* a byword in the past, present and straight into the future!

There is one more gesture that needs to be done. Michael has been described as the "King of Pop", or a member of entertainment royalty, or an icon of the music industry. Now is the time to bestow a fitting title that is all inclusive; one that not only is given for his talent and contribution to the planet, but for being consistent in sounding the same message over the years.

It is an honor to bestow upon Michael Jackson the title of "American Master". Our world is willing and able to capture more enjoyment and knowledge from this gifted spokesman and representative of our time. Our hopes and prayers are that he will continue to nourish the planet and delight us with more of his talent in the future.

Photo Courtesy of MJJ Productions

Chapter 5:

The Master Manifests His Gift to the Planet

"It is true that you only get out of something what you put into it."
Michael Jackson

It was delivered in a brown envelope. It was addressed very carefully. The label carried the Moonwalk logo. It was opened, and there it was: the discography and awards that Michael has received throughout his years of exhibiting his talent and the sharing of his craft to the planet.

The receiver of the gift turned the pages of the printed material very carefully. The contents were studied. It was far more than what appeared in printed form on the pages. It displayed the history of a man. As the pages were studied with great care, a warm feeling encased the body of the receiver. Having the opportunity to receive such information, the maximum benefit was to be gained.

There is a reciprocal relationship between the giver and receiver of such a gift. In keeping with Michael's thought that one gets out of something what one puts into it, one can see all the effort, the sacrifices, manifested for his personal accomplishments. It also discloses the gifts he produced for his fellow brothers and sisters on the planet.

In the desire to capture the essence of the offering, the material transcended the printed words. It was taken to the next step of the invisible vibrations of his music. One by one, the selections were listened to and transformed into the world of the artist and listener -- the giver and the receiver. It filled the room with its lessons, beauty, and touched the soul.

On the following pages is the very same material that came in the brown envelope and reached the welcome hands of the receiver. However, it was given to not only one person, but to the world in which all of us reside.

In truth, it is much more than merely a list of songs in the form of a discography and awards. It gives the history of the master and his continuing desire to increase the innate ability of enhancing one's talent and thought process, thereby affecting the destiny of mankind.

As a receiver of such information, what are you going to do with the accomplishments the master attained in his craft? It is totally dependent upon what you are looking for in life and understanding what you are seeking is what you will find. The pages note not only the number of awards but depict the quality of life that Michael attains.

In viewing the material, it can take you back to the time in your life that you first heard the selections. It can recall a part of your own history and development. What happened to you throughout the years? The outstanding feature, and the message of the master, is to take your talent to the next level. On the pages listing his awards and manifestations of his music, Michael illustrated consistency in his endeavors by the example of his manifestations. He challenged himself to greater and greater heights by using the gift of his talent.

The record of such accomplishments is not the end result of his creativity. It is at the heart of this astute individual. The heart is always at the center of the invisible and intuitive creation; it's where it always commences. It is the vital part where the beat and breath of life exists.

To get the essence of the master's manifestation and to assist the reader in obtaining the maximum message, the offerings of Michael Jackson are placed at its proper position in the book: its heart and in the center of its message, where the inspiration is at its rightful place. It will serve as a closure to the first part of the book and assist in the development of the second segment.

Photo Courtesy of MJJ Productions

The Musical
Manifestations
of
Michael Jackson

What are the intrinsic characteristics of a master? Those people fortunate enough to see the 1996 World Music Awards in Monaco received a clue when Michael Jackson made a grand sweep of the honors, based on world wide sales of his manifestations.

Masters appear before presidents, princes and princesses. Once again, Michael was surrounded by royalty. He sat front row center during the Awards, and was flanked by both Princess Stephanie and Prince Albert, who each personally presented him with awards.

Perhaps the most outstanding feature of the evening was when he performed *Earth Song* before the creme-de-la-creme of the musical industry. The audience's reaction included calling out his name, holding their cheeks in the palms of their hands, tears streaming down their faces, rubbing their eyes, and clenching their fists in wonderment of the performance and performer they were witnessing. This spectacle was not simply about his music; it depicted the essence of the master by his profound, direct and strong display of movement, dance, and outstretched arms.

What was his message? To have his musical talent serve all people over all the world. A master always sets the correct example. He loves, adores, and is concerned with all nationalities and ethnic origins. His messages, he said, are not intended to be offensive to any ethnic group, but that, through his music, his messages are to show the iniquities of mankind.

How do you know when you see a master? In the short video mix introduced by Princess Stephanie, celebrities including Gregory Peck perhaps expressed it best.

"...He is what the French like to call a *monstre sacre*, a sacred monster, someone who's completely unique."

"...He is probably the most famous person on the planet, God help him. When Michael Jackson sings, it is with the voice of angels, and when his feet move, you can see God dancing."

The awards Michael received in Monaco are an example of how the world appreciates the master. They acknowledge the highest expression of gifts between the giver and the receiver -- a record-breaking total of more than 500 million albums sold worldwide.

Complete Discography

Jackson Five

1969
I Want You Back
Zip a Dee Doo Dah
Nobody
Can You Remember
Standing in the Shadows of Love
You've Changed
My Cherie Amour
Chained
(I Know) I'm Losing You
Stand
Born to Love You
Who's Lovin' You
ABC
The Young Folks
Sing a Simple Song
The Love You Save
I Found That Girl
One More Chance

1969-1970
(Come Round Here) I'm the One You Need
Don't Know Why I Love You
Never Had a Dream Come True
True Love Can Be Beautiful
La La (Means I Love You)
I'll Bet You

<u>1970</u>
One Day I'll Marry You
Darling Dear
Mama's Pearl
Ask the Lonely
Santa Claus is Comin' to Town
Christmas Won't Be the Same This Year
Have Yourself a Merry Little Christmas
The Christmas Song
Up On a Housetop
Frosty the Snowman
The Little Drummer Boy
Rudolph the Red-Nosed Reindeer
Give Love on Christmas Day
Someday at Christmas
I Saw Mommy Kissing Santa Claus
I Ain't Gonna Eat Out My Heart Anymore
I'll Be There
I'm So Happy
Ready or Not, Here I Come
Oh How Happy
Bridge Over Troubled Water
Can I See You in the Morning
Goin' Back to Indiana
How Funky Is Your Chicken
Reach In
The Love I Saw in You Was Just a Mirage

1971

Medley: Mama's Pearl/Walk On By/The Love You Save
Medley: I'll Be There/Feelin' Alright
Never Can Say Goodbye
I Will Find a Way
If I Have to Move a Mountain
She's Good
Love Song
Maybe Tomorrow
The Wall
Petals
Sixteen Candles
(We've Got) Blue Skies
My Little Baby
It's Great to Be Here
Honey Chile
Just Because I Love You
Penny Arcade
I Want You Back (Live)
Maybe Tomorrow (Live)
The Day Basketball Was Saved (Live)
Stand (Live)
I Want to Take You Higher (Live)
Feelin' Alright (Live)
Medley: The Love You Save/Walk On By (Live)
Goin' Back to Indiana (Live)
You Made Me What I Am
Sugar Daddy

1972
To Know
Little Bitty Pretty One
Lookin' Through the Windows
Doctor My Eyes
Ain't Nothing Like the Real Thing
Don't Let Your Baby Catch You
E-ne-me-ne-mi-ne-moe
Don't Want To See Tomorrow
Children of The Light
I Can Only Give You Love
I Was Made to Love Her
Corner of the Sky
I Can't Quit Your Love
Touch
Hallelujah Day

1972-1973
Skywriter
The Boogie Man
Uppermost
World of Sunshine
Ooh, I'd Love to Be With You

1973

We're Gonna Have a Good Time (Japan Live)
Lookin' Through the Windows (Japan Live)
Got to Be There (Japan Live)
Daddy's Home (Japan Live)
Superstition (Japan Live)
Ben (Japan Live)
Papa Was a Rollin' Stone (Japan Live)
That's How Love Goes (Japan Live)
Never Can Say Goodbye (Japan Live)
Ain't That Peculiar (Japan Live)
I Wanna Be Where You Are (Japan Live)
I Am Love Part 1
I Am Love Part 2
It's Too Late to Change the Time
Get It Together
Dancing Machine
She's a Rhythm Child
The Life of the Party
We're Gonna Change Our Style
Teenage Symphony
I Hear a Symphony
Give Me Half a Chance
You're Good for Me
I Like You the Way You Are
Whatever You Got, I Want
What You Don't Know
It All Begins and Ends With Love

Breezy
Call of the Wild
Time Explosion
The Eternal Light
If I Don't Love You This Way
The Mirrors of My Mind
Don't Say Goodbye Again
Reflections
Hum Along and Dance
Mama I Gotta Brand New Thing
You Need Love Like I Do

1974

All I Do Is Think of You
Forever Came Today
Moving Violation
Especially for Me
Honey Love

1974-1975

Body Language

1975

Joyful Jukebox Music
Window Shopping
You're My Best Friend, My Love
Love Is the Thing You Need
Make Tonight All Mine
Pride & Joy
Through Thick and Thin
We're Here to Entertain You

The Jacksons

1976
Enjoy Yourself
Show You the Way To Go
Think Happy
Style of Live
Blues Away
Strength of One Man

1976-1977
Keep On Dancing
Living Together
Jump for Joy
Good Times
Dreamer
Even Though You're Gone
Heaven Knows I Love You, Girl
Man of War
Find Me a Girl

1977

Goin' Places
Music's Takin' Over
Different Kind of Lady
Do What You Wanna

1978

Blame It on the Boogie
Push Me Away
Things I Do for You
Shake Your Body (Down to the Ground)
Destiny
Bless His Soul
All Night Dancin'
That's What You Get (For Being Polite)
Can You Feel It
Lovely One
Your Ways
Everybody
Heartbreak Hotel
Time Waits for No One
Walk Right Now
Give It Up
Wondering Who

1981
Opening (Live)
Can You Feel It (Live)
Things I Do for You (Live)
Off the Wall (Live)
Ben (Live)
Heartbreak Hotel (Live)
She's Out of My Life (Live)
I Want You Back (Live)
Never Can Say Goodbye (Live)
Got to Be There (Live)
I Want You Back (Live)
ABC (Live)
The Love You Save (Live)
I'll Be There (Live)
Rock With You (Live)
Lovely One (Live)
Workin' Day and Night (Live)
Don't Stop (Live)
Shake Your Body (Live)

1984
Torture
Wait
One More Chance
The Hurt
Be Not Always
State of Shock
We Can Change the World
Body
Time Out for the Burglar

Michael Jackson

1971

You Can Cry on My Shoulder
Got to Be There
Maria
Rockin' Robin
Love Is Here and Now You're Gone
I Wanna Be Where You Are
We've Got a Good Thing Going
Ain't No Sunshine
In Our Small Way
Girl Don't Take Your Love From Me
Wings of My Love
You've Got a Friend

1972

Ben
Greatest Show on Earth
People Make the World Go Around
What Goes Around Comes Around
Everybody's Somebody's Fool
My Girl
Shoo-bee-doo-be-doo-da-day
Morning Glow
With a Child's Heart
Little Christmas Tree

1973
Melodie
All the Things You Are
Music and Me
Happy
Too Young
Doggin' Around
Euphoria
Johnny Raven
To Make My Father Proud
If'n I Was God
Here I Am
You've Really Got a Hold on Me
Touch the One You Love
Don't Let It Get You Down
Girl You're So Together
Farewell My Summer Love
Call on Me

1974
We're Almost There
Just a Little Bit of You
One Day in Your Life
You Are There
Dear Michael
We've Got Forever
Take Me Back
Cinderella Stay Awhile
Dapper-Dan
I'll Come Home to You

1978-79
Off The Wall
Girlfriend
It's the Falling in Love
She's Out of My Life
I Can't Help It
Don't Stop 'Til You Get Enough
Working Day and Night
Get on the Floor
Rock With You
Off the Wall
Burn This Disco Out

1982-83
Thriller
The Girl Is Mine
Someone in the Dark
Wanna Be Startin' Somethin'
Beat It
Billie Jean
Thriller
Lady in My Life
Human Nature
Pretty Young Thing
Say Say Say
This Is the Man

1987
Bad
The Way You Make Me Feel
Bad
Speed Demon
Liberian Girl
Another Part of Me
Dirty Diana
Smooth Criminal
Just Good Friends
Man in the Mirror
I Just Can't Stop Loving You

1991
Dangerous
Black or White
Dangerous
Gone Too Soon
In the Closet
Heal the World
Jam
Why You Wanna Trip on Me
She Drives Me Wild
Remember the Time
Can't Let Her Get Away
Give in To Me
Who Is It?
Keep the Faith
Will You Be There?

1995
HIStory: Past, Present & Future, Book 1
Scream
(Duet with Michael Jackson and Janet Jackson)
They Don't Care About Us
Stranger in Moscow
This Time Around
Earth Song
D.S.
Money
Come Together
You Are Not Alone
Childhood (Theme from "Free Willy 2")
Tabloid Junkie
2 Bad
HIStory
Little Susie
Smile

Michael Jackson's Awards

1970

NAACP IMAGE AWARDS   *Best Singing Group*

1971

GRAMMY AWARDS   *Best Pop song, "ABC"*
NAACP IMAGE AWARDS   *Best Singing Group*

1972

BILLBOARD   *Top Singles Artist*
                    Top Singles Male
GOLDEN GLOBE   *"Ben"*
NAACP IMAGE AWARDS   *Best Singing Group*
U.S. CONGRESS   *Special Commendation for Positive*
                    Role Models

1979

GRAMMY AWARDS   *Best R&B Performance, "Don't Stop*
                    'Til You Get Enough"

1980

AMERICAN MUSIC AWARDS   *Favorite Male Soul Artist*
                    Favorite Soul Album, "Off the Wall"
                    Favorite Soul Single, "Don't Stop
                    'Til You Get Enough"
BILLBOARD AWARDS   *Top Black Artist*
                    Top Black Album, "Off the Wall"
CASHBOX   *Top Soul Album, "Off the Wall"*
NAACP IMAGE AWARDS   *Best Singing Group*

1981

AMERICAN MUSIC AWARDS   *Favorite Male Vocalist -Soul/R&B*
                                         Favorite Album Soul/R&B

BRITISH PHONOGRAPHIC   *"Off the Wall" Album*
    INDUSTRY AWARDS
NAACP IMAGE AWARDS   *Best Singing Group*

1983

BLACK GOLD AWARDS   *Top Male Vocalist*
                                         Best Video Performance
                                         Best Single of the Year
                                         Best Album
BILLBOARD AWARDS   *Pop Artist of the Year*
                                         Black Artist of the Year
                                         Pop Album of the Year
                                         Pop Album Artist
                                         Pop Singles Artist
                                         Pop Male Album
                                         Pop Male Singles
                                         Black Albums Artist
                                         Black Singles Artist
                                         Black Album
                                         Dance/Disco Artist
                                         Dance/Disco 12" LP, "Billie Jean"
                                         Dance/Disco 12" LP, "Beat It"
BILLBOARD AWARD VIDEOS   *Best Video*
                                         Best Male Performance
                                         Best Use of Video to Enhance
                                              Artist's Image
                                         Best Use of Video to Enhance
                                              Artist's Song
                                         Best Choreography

CASHBOX
Number One Male Artist
Pop Single "Billie Jean"
Male - Single Artist
Black Album
Pop Album
Black Male Artist
Black Male - Singles Artist
Black Single, "Billie Jean"

ROLLING STONE
Readers - Artist of the Year
Readers - Soul Artist
Readers - Video, "Beat It"
Readers - Producers
Critics - Artist of the Year
Critics - Video, "Beat It"
Critics - Male Vocalist
Critics - Soul Artist

AUSTRALIA
Album of the Year
Single of the Year

BRAZIL
Int'l Artist of the Year

GREECE
Record of the Year

HOLLAND
Album of the Year

ITALY
Artist of the Year

JAPAN
Artist of the Year
Male Vocalist
Album of the Year

SPAIN
Most Important Foreign Album

UNITED KINGDOM
Album of the Year
Artist of the Year

1984

AMERICAN MUSIC AWARDS
Special Award of Merit
Favorite Male Vocalist - Pop/Rock
Favorite Single - Pop/Rock
Favorite Album - Pop/Rock
Favorite Video - Pop/Rock
Favorite Male Vocalist - Soul/R&B
Favorite Video - Soul/R&B

AMERICAN VIDEO AWARDS	*Best Long Form Video*
	Best Home Video
BILLBOARD AWARDS	*Top Album*
CRYSTAL GLOBE AWARDS	*Exceeding Sales Past 5 Million*
EBONY MAGAZINE AWARDS	
GRAMMY AWARDS	
	Producer of the Year
	Album of the Year "Thriller"
	Record of the Year "Beat It"
	Best Male Rock Vocal
	Performance, "Beat It"
	Best New R&B Song, "Billie Jean"
	Best Male Pop Performance
	Best Recording for Children
	"E.T., The Extra Terrestrial" Album
	Best Male Pop Performance
GUINNESS BOOK OF RECORDS	*Best Selling Album of All Time*
HOTEL ROYAL PLAZA	*Presentation Casement "37 Gold*
	Gold & Platinum Discs"
HOLLYWOOD STAR	*Hall of Fame Solo Star for*
	Michael Jackson
MTV AWARDS	*Best Overall Video*
	Best Choreography
	Viewers Choice Award
PEOPLE'S CHOICE AWARDS	*Best All Around Entertainer*
	of the Year
NAACP IMAGE AWARDS	*H. Claude Hodson Medal of Freedom*
NARM	*Gift of Music Award*
	Best Selling Album and Single
	Best Home Video "Making of
	Thriller"
UNITED KINGDOM	*Presentation Casement of*
	Platinum Disc 1985 "Thriller"

1985

GRAMMY AWARDS	*Best Home Video*
	"Making of Thriller"

1986

AMERICAN MUSIC AWARDS	Award of Appreciation
	Song of the Year "We Are the World"
GRAMMY AWARDS	Song of the Year "We Are the World"
	Record of the Year
	Best Pop Performance, Duo or Group
	Best Music Video Short Film
GUINNESS BOOK OF RECORDS	Largest Ever Endorsement for Production
PEOPLE'S CHOICE AWARDS	"We Are the World"

1987

BRAVO MAGAZINE	Silver Otto Award

1988

AMERICAN MUSIC AWARDS	Favorite Single - Soul/R&B
BILLBOARD AWARDS	Top Black Artist
BLUES & SOUL	Outstanding Artist of the Year
	Best Live Show of 1988
BRAVO MAGAZINE	Gold Otto Award
EBONY MAGAZINE	American Black Achievement Award
FORBES	#1 Entertainer of the Year
GUILD HALL PARTY	Presentation of Sword to Commemorate "Bad" Tour
MTV VANGUARD	Outstanding Contribution to Music Video Production
NAACP IMAGE AWARDS	Best Male Artist "Bad" Single
	Best Album "Bad"
	Leonard Carter Humanitarian
SOUL TRAIN	R&B Album of the Year
	Best Male Single of the Year
WEMBLEY STADIUM	For Seven Sell Out Record Breaking Shows

1989

AMERICAN MUSIC AWARDS	Special Award of Achievement
AMERICAN DANCE AWARD	

BET	Award, Success of "Bad" Tour
BILLBOARD AWARDS	Number One Black Artist
	"Thriller" #1 Album Pop/R&B
RAVO MAGAZINE	Bronze Otto Award
BRE AWARDS	Triple Crown Award, King of Pop, Rock & Soul
	Video of the Year
BRITISH TV INDUSTRY AWARDS	Artist of the Decade
BRITISH PHONOGRAPHIC INDUSTRY AWARDS	Video of the Year
BRITISH ACADEMY OF MUSIC AWARDS	Best International Male Artist
CASHBOX	Video Pioneer
CRITIC'S CHOICE AWARD	Best Video
ENTERTAINMENT TONIGHT	Most Important Entertainer of the Decade
FRIDAY NIGHT VIDEO	Greatest Artist of the Decade
	Number One Artist
FORBES	#1 Entertainer of the Year ($)
GARDNER STREET ELEMENTARY SCHOOL	Most Famous Alumnus Renamed School Auditorium
MTV AWARDS	Video Vanguard Award - "Thriller" The Greatest Video in the History of the World
NATIONAL URBAN COALITION	Humanitarian Award
PEOPLE'S CHOICE AWARDS	Favorite Music Video "SmoothCriminal"
ROLLING STONE MAGAZINE	"Thriller" Video of the Decade
SOUL TRAIN AWARDS	Heritage Award, R&B Contemporary
	1st Annual Sammy Davis Jr. Award
U.K TV SHOW	Good-by to the 80's Award
VANITY FAIR	Artist of the Decade
VIDEO SOFTWARE DEALERS ASSOC.	"Moonwalker" As Favorite Musical Video
WORLD MUSIC AWARDS	Hall of Fame
	Lifetime Achievement in Video
	Viewers Choice # 1 Video "Dirty Diana"

1990

AMERICAN CINEMA AWARDS	*Entertainer of the Decade*
EMMY NOMINEE	*Composing Sammy David Jr. 60th Anniversary Song "You Were There"*
BMI	*Inaugural: 1st Michael Jackson Award of Achievement*
BOY SCOUTS OF AMERICA	*Good Scout Humanitarian*
CAPITAL CHILDREN'S MUSEUM	*Humanitarian Award*
GRAMMY AWARDS	*Best Video "Leave Me Alone"*
MUSIC CONNECTION	*Man of the Decade*
SONY ENTERTAINMENT (CBS RECORDS)	*Top Selling Artist of the Decade*
SOUL TRAIN AWARDS	*Artist of the Decade*
VANITY FAIR	*Most Popular Artist in the History of Show Business*
WHITE HOUSE RECOGNITION PRESIDENT GEORGE BUSH	*Artist of the Decade*

1991

MTV AWARDS	*Renames its Video Vanguard Award to Michael Jackson Video Vanguard Award in his honor*

1992

BRAVO MAGAZINE	*Gold Otto Award*
GABON, AFRICA	*National Honor of Merit Award*
NABOB	*Lifetime Achievement Award*
OPERATION ONE TO ONE AWARD	
PRESIDENT OF THE U.S. GEORGE BUSH	*Point of Light Ambassador*

1993

AMERICAN MUSIC AWARDS	*Pop/Rock Album "Dangerous"* *Best Soul/R&B Single for "Remember the Time"* *Special Int'l Artist Award for record sales and humanitarian efforts around the world.*

BRAVO MAGAZINE	Gold Otto Award
BMI AWARDS	"Black or White" and "Remember the Time", two of the Most Performed Songs of the Year
GRAMMY AWARDS	Living Legend Award
GUINNESS BOOK OF WORLD RECORDS	Lifetime Achievement Award for his unprecedented world records in the world of entertainment
NAACP IMAGE AWARDS	25th Silver Anniversary Entertainer of the Year Award
	Outstanding Music Video "Black or White"
SOUL TRAIN AWARDS	1993 Humanitarian of the Year Award
	Best R&B Single "Remember the Time"
	Best R&B Album "Dangerous"
WORLD MUSIC AWARDS	Best Selling American Artist
	World's Best Selling Pop Artist
	World's Best Selling Artist of the Era

1994

BRAVO MAGAZINE	Gold Otto Award
CRENSHAW COMMUNITY YOUTH AND ARTS FOUNDATION	Humanitarian Award
SMASH HITS AWARDS	Best Male Vocalist
POP ROCK MAGAZINE	Favorite Singer of the Year

1995

BRAVO MAGAZINE	Gold Otto Award
INSTITUTE OF MUSICAL ART	Innovator's Award
N.A.R.M.	Harry Chapin Memorial Humanitarian Award
POPCORN MAGAZINE	Artist of the Decade Award

1996

AMERICAN MUSIC AWARDS	*Favorite Male Artist Pop/Rock*
ARK TRUST GENESIS AWARDS	*Doris Day Award, "Earth Song"*
Video	
BILLBOARD AWARDS	
BLOCKBUSTER AWARDS	*Favorite Pop Male Artist*
BRIT AWARDS	*Artist of a Generation*
DENMARK GRAMMY AWARDS	*Best International Male Artist*
	Best International Album
GERARDMER'S FANTASTIC ARTS	
FESTIVAL, FRANCE	*Best Video, "Earth Song"*
GRAMMY AWARDS	*Best Video - Short Form*
IRMA AWARDS, IRELAND	*Best International Male Artist*
MTV AWARDS	
NAACP AWARDS	
SOUL TRAIN AWARDS	*Lifetime Achievement Award*
WORLD MUSIC AWARDS	*Best Selling Male Artist*
	Best Selling American Artist
	Best Selling R&B Artist
	Best Selling Record of All Time,
	"Thriller"
	Best Selling Artist of All Time

U.S.A. Solo & Group Awards

Michael Jackson

Got To Be There	Gold	Single
Ben	Platinum/Gold	Single
Rockin' Robin	Gold	Single
Don't Stop 'Til U Get Enuf	Platinum/Gold	Single
Rock With You	Platinum/Gold	Single
Off The Wall	Gold	Single
She's Out of My Life	Gold	Single
The Girl Is Mine	Gold	Single
Billie Jean	Platinum/Gold	Single
Beat It	Platinum/Gold	Single
Say Say Say	Platinum/Gold	Single
I Just Can't...Loving You	Gold	Single
We Are The World	M-Plat/Plat/Gold	Single
Ben	Gold	Album
Off The Wall	M-Plat/Plat/Gold	Album
Thriller	M-Plat/Plat/Gold	Album
Bad	M-Plat/Plat/Gold	Album
Dangerous	M-Plat/Plat/Gold	Album
HIStory	M-Plat/Plat/Gold	Album

Jacksons

Enjoy Yourself	Platinum/Gold	Single
Shake Your Body	Platinum/Gold	Single
State of Shock	Gold	Single
The Jacksons	Platinum/Gold	Album
Destiny	Platinum/Gold	Album
Triumph	M-Plat/Plat/Gold	Album
Victory	M-Plat/Plat/Gold	Album

Jackson Five

I Want You Back	Platinum/Gold	Single
ABC	Platinum/Gold	Single
The Love You Share	Platinum/Gold	Single
I'll Be There	Platinum/Gold	Single
Never Can Say Goodbye	Gold	Single
Mama's Pearl	Gold	Single
Sugar Daddy	Gold	Single
Dancing Machine	Gold	Single
Diana Ross Presents	Gold	Album
ABC	Gold	Album
The Third Album	Gold	Album
Goin' Back to Indiana	Gold	Album
Looking Thru the Window	Gold	Album
Dancing Machine	Gold	Album

U.S.A. Compact Disc Awards

HIStory	Platinum/Gold
Dangerous	Platinum/Gold
Thriller	Platinum/Gold
Bad	Platinum/Gold
Off The Wall	Gold
18 Greatest Hits	Gold
The Making of Thriller	Gold
Moonwalker	Platinum/Gold
The Legend Continues	Gold

United Kingdom Compact Disc Awards

Thriller	Platinum/Gold
Bad	Platinum/Gold
Off The Wall	Gold
18 Greatest Hits	Gold
The Making of Thriller	Platinum/Gold

United Kingdom Album Awards

18 Greatest Hits	Platinum/Gold
Destiny	Gold
Triumph	Platinum/Gold
Victory	Platinum/Gold
Ben	Gold
Farewell My Summer Love	Gold
Best of Michael Jackson	Gold
One Day in Your Life	Gold
The Michael Jackson Mix	Gold
Michael/Diana Love Songs	Gold

United Kingdom Singles Awards

Want You Back	Gold
ABC	Gold
Show You the Way to Go	Gold
Shake Your Body	Gold
Can You Feel It	Gold
Ben	Gold
Rockin' Robin	Gold
I Just Can't...You	Gold
One Day in Your Life	Gold

International Record Awards

Multi–Platinum/Platinum/Gold Singles

Don't Stop 'Til You Get Enough	Australia	Italy
	Japan	Spain
	U.K.	

Rock With You	Canada	Denmark
	France	Holland
	Italy	New Zealand
	U.K.	

Beat It	Australia	Belgium
	Canada	France
	New Zealand	
	U.K.	

Say Say Say	Germany	Holland
	Italy	Spain
	U.K.	

She's Out of My Life	France	Germany
	Holland	Italy
	Spain	U.K.

The Master
Confronts the Issues
of the World

Photo Courtesy of MJJ Productions

Introduction:

The Master Relates to Children

In the first section of the book, we discussed the characteristics of the masters and how Michael Jackson exhibits his mastership through his intuitive understanding of the universe.

In the second section, some issues facing our generation, and their solutions, will be discussed. While referring to Michael, it incorporates some of the author's interpretations and insights resulting from her long tenure working with children; her years of reading, research, and studying human behavior; and her relentless struggle to enhance her own understanding and quality of life.

The most important reason for discussing children is that they are still free from the grasp of arbitrary rules and codes of society.

Chapter 6:

A World of Mastery

"No one should have to suffer, especially the children."
Michael Jackson

If we understand the thought process and creativity of the masters, we can find the solution to the problems that we are confronting in our generation.

The equation between the giver and receiver is elementary, and basic in understanding our primary purpose in life. First of all, we have to realize that all of the inhabitants of the earth are the receivers of two gifts: (1) The gift of life; and (2) A home on which to live during our earthly journey. The gifts include everything that is necessary to our survival: (1) The atmosphere which gives us the air we need in order to breath; (2) The sun, which offers us warmth and light; and (3) The moon, which controls the ebb and flow of the tides.

Every day we take a trip by completing one rotation on an invisible axis, giving us our days and nights. We are also moving at a very fast rate of speed as we complete each journey around the sun, giving us the four seasons in a year.

The planet furnishes soil to grow our food. We are given water, which is constantly recycled, to nourish the plants and provide an element that we need for our own bodies. It reveals its history by tall mountains and canyons, lakes and rivers. It truly is a wonderful home with tropical plants and lush trees.

We were given the perfect body to adapt beautifully to the landscape. All parts of our physical body work in unison to give us continued life. We have our limbs to walk the various pathways; our senses to see, hear, smell and eat. To keep our bodies in healthy order for growth and maintenance, we have organs which benefit when we use our environment properly. Our physical being is truly a miracle.

There is also another component all humans possess, which is perhaps more magnificent, and that is our invisible self. We can call it the soul, the spiritual self, or in more common terms, the core of our being. This is the part of us that has the ability to manifest in the physical world by the use of intuition, inspiration, and thought.

Our physical bodies are in harmony with the functions of the planet and, therefore, are limited by boundaries. The invisible part of our being is dependent on the strong pull of other forces; it is not limited by physical boundaries. It is therefore more adaptable to universal law and creation. Being invisible, it draws on other invisible counterparts such as our emotions and feelings. In order to manifest, we have to act on these stimuli by the use of our brain power that has the ability to transform them into the physical form.

Michael Jackson believes that we have the brain power to give physical form to our creativity. The intuition comes first and then the idea is formulated by the logical side of our brain. Most importantly, through the creative process, we learn how to expand on a primary idea and take it to a higher level.

This is continually apparent in the sciences and arts. One just has to look at technology to grasp the concept. Each generation is expanding and developing from the knowledge of the previous generation.

In a physical world, we are quite adept at using these principles until we come to interpersonal relationships. Why is this? It could be that we think that we have this thing called "living" down so pat that we form all kinds of systems, techniques, and categories. We become synthesized and believe that by applying the same codes, we might keep a sibilance of order and the status quo, but it isn't keeping abreast with individual creativity. It may be for some people who excel and rise above the crowd, but not for the majority of the populace.

The real crux of the problem is that we do not recognize the talents that all of us possess. This is bad enough when adults don't recognize their own inherent power of creativity, but it becomes compounded when adults don't let children experience the creative force that lies patiently waiting for expression.

Children learn at a very early age how to conform to the family and how to please parents, teachers, and their friends. We then wonder why they submit to peer pressure!

True expansion comes from the unleashing of ideas. How would a master solve some of the dilemmas in the world today by the use of the creative force? All the world knows where Michael Jackson would start. He would start with the children. Naturally! Of course! Maybe not.

Children learn from example. Where do they get their first examples? They get their experience in the early years of development from the family. The parents are the primary caretakers, and the children learn to please them very quickly because to show displeasure could mean that their desires, or more importantly, their needs, may not be met.

Using the creative process, let's reverse it. Let's allow the child to inform the parents what he would like to do. Surprisingly, the child would get enough food and sleep. Have you ever watched a child play and play, and then watch him become very quiet and fall immediately to sleep? You know the pattern. Pow, one, two, three. He's out like a light!

Photo Courtesy of MJJ Productions

What would happen if we carried that same idea into what we call formal learning? Children know at a very early age what they can do best and where their talents lay. We know this by talking, reading, or studying with prodigies.   They play the piano at three, read, or are extremely mechanical at a very early age. Michael was intelligent and one could see how easily he grasped knowledge. His mother was definitely a nurturing factor when it came to his love of music.

Exposure to life's experiences enhances the creative process. The answer, as always, comes from education. Before we can educate the young, we first have to educate ourselves on the best ways to instill knowledge.

If we believe a child knows when he is ready to accomplish the physical world, it would follow that he would show an interest in his creativity, and in the invisible world, which includes morals and ethics. Every parent has gone through the various "no" or "why" stages - from toddlers to adolescents!

Earlier, it was mentioned that parents shouldn't wait too long in discussing delicate subjects. Due to AIDS and the sexual revolution, parents think that the answer is in educating their children by explaining "safe sex". When the family is close, and the children have been taught that their bodies are a miraculous creation to be taken care of properly; when the parents are good role models, and there is good communication and a closeness and caring attitude; and when the children are valued as special and unique individuals; then they will grow up knowing how to honor and protect their bodies. They will learn that their body is the one thing that they can control, including the manner in which they choose to use or share the most intimate part of themselves.

Feelings need to be validated, whether they are right or wrong, before progress can be made. First, this is a non-judgmental approach. Second, whether or not the feelings are proper, correct, or sound, they are very real to the person experiencing them. It is necessary to know first of all why a person is acting in a certain manner. Knowing the reasoning behind the action, alternate choices can be offered to correct the thinking process into a positive mode of behavior.   Adults using this technique are exhibiting what psychologists call "Behavior Modification".

There are many ways to expand knowledge. Experience is not only a very good teacher, but practical as well. Through trial and error, we can learn what will work and what doesn't. We can learn from the experiences of others. This is the primary reason for this book.

Michael Jackson has accomplished more in a mere thirty eight years than most people could even contemplate doing in a lifetime, let alone actually manifest such awesome achievements. However, he reveals some very practical examples.

Earlier, it was mentioned that Michael enlisted the assistance of some gang members for his short film, *Beat It*. He commented that they were basically a good group, and that all they wanted was to be heard. Michael gave them respect for the individuals they were, and that respect was returned by them. What we give, we will receive. There was good communication on the set; each side learning something from the other: the act of giving and receiving.

Being receptive requires being totally open and, at times, extremely vulnerable. Listening to one another is a way of learning through the example of the thought process. Good listening is an art, and contrary to opinion, is not a passive activity. Hearing is passive; listening is active. It requires taking in information from another source, analyzing, and effectively applying the new information.

Thinking about this concept reminded me of two examples with an eight year old boy in one of the youth homes where I was employed. One night, I went into this young resident's room and he was packing to leave because he was very upset. He was throwing his clothes off the hangers and onto the floor in very rapid succession.

Instead of scolding him, I walked over to him and asked him if anything was wrong. He loudly told me he was mad at another employee, that he hated this place, and he was leaving. I explained that I understood, that living away from his parents wasn't easy to do, and that his mother really loved him, but was unable to care for him. I told him that I was really "scared" about his safety.

I asked him if he had figured out how he was going to survive, to which he replied that he would take some blankets and find a place to sleep. I then asked him how he was going to get food. He said that he would go to the store. I asked him if he had any money. I went and got my purse and showed him that I just had a couple of dollars, not even enough for a box of Cheerios and milk! He said he would go to the bank. I asked him if he had put money into the bank; otherwise, he couldn't get money out. I explained how banks operate.

While I was talking with him, I was helping him pack. I was doing this very slowly and could tell that he was getting very sleepy and not helping much. I made the suggestion that he go to bed and he could think about his departure. I tucked him in, gave him a hug, and told him that I hoped that he would still be here when I came to work the next day. He called me to come back to his bed and whispered in my ear, "I think I want to stay here. Could you read me a story before I go to sleep?"

Another incident I had with this child was when he was in the recreational room. Again, he was angry, throwing books, toys, and the cushions from the sofa, onto the floor. When I came into the room, I asked him what he was doing. "I'm mad," he said. "Oh," I said, "Well you're not too mad because you made quite a mess, but you haven't broken the television or turned over the fish tank!"

He laughed and told me that he was mad because his friend couldn't come over. I said that it was dinner time and, if he could wait until after dinner, we would call his friend and see if he could spend all afternoon the next day. He thought that would be great if we could go out to the park with him. We called his friend after dinner and they had a very good time.

What transpired in these two examples is that the child's feelings were validated by the adult. He was showing by his actions that he felt no one was interested in how he felt. Good communication took place between the adult and child, with the adult being non-judgmental and elaborating on the child's thinking process. The child, in turn, made his own choice which, naturally, was going to be the correct one and in his best interest.

Through finding a mutual place of agreement, the situation could be turned around. A master's quality in changing behavior is in his ability to see a need and fulfill that need in an interesting and effective way. This takes intuition, thought, and creativity, whether it be a song, dance, or an issue facing our society.

In discussing Michael Jackson, his picture of depicting a wounded world by the placement of a bandaid on the earth is a profound illustration of the plight of the planet. Society has a tendency to concern itself with the outward manifestation without really getting at the internal causes both on an individual and global basis. We use people as examples and then think, by the use of force or punishment, we can correct the cause. We feel that by doing this, and the use of retaliation, people are going to conform.

This is not how human nature operates. Our survival tendencies always kick into operation when we think we are in danger. This includes any attack on our physical or emotional well-being. It's strange how we teach our children that two wrongs never make a right. Yet, we don't seem to use this mentality in attempting to solve many of the issues of today. Our youth is learning from this example.

The young find solutions to their problems in the subtle actions of adults. An example is the manner in which our law enforcement agencies fulfill their duties. The primary duty of our police forces is to protect all of the citizens of their jurisdiction. How are they illustrating to the public the best method of maintaining law? By their demeanor, uniforms, handcuffs and guns, are they giving us the correct message of maintaining a peaceful and harmonious environment? Are we giving the proper message to young people? Granted, guns might be necessary for the protection of the police and some individuals, but should they be displayed in such a conspicuous manner? The idea as a deterrent may be valid, but is it giving some of our youth the proper message?

Many of the toy guns have been removed from major toy retailers. The reason that this is being done is that the police are seeing youth performing a crime and using these toy guns to frighten people. In some instances, the police assume that they are real guns, and respond by shooting the youth displaying such a weapon, even if it is a toy.

The removal of toy guns from stores is a good start. Here again, though, we have to look at the cause of such behavior by both parties. The use of a toy gun represents an example set by society. In cases when the police mistake a toy gun as a real weapon, they respond by using their guns. This is a classic case where two wrongs don't make a right. The person who enacted the crime was wrong; the police who mistook the replica of a gun were also wrong.

A solution on the part of the police might be in using the intuitive source. It is certain that the victim did not fire a gun. In finding the true solutions to the problems of our society, like the masters, we must look at the scope of the situation and then break it down to specifics. After doing those two things, we can then make a conscious decision.

Photo Courtesy of MJJ Productions

Chapter 7:

The Master Identifies the Real Issue

"Hear the truth before you label or condemn me."
Michael Jackson

The contents of the book have been based on factual information and when an interpretation is given, it has been stated as such. At this time, the author is going to write about two experiences she had with children.

The first account has to do with what happens when an infraction became apparent to the general public, and shows how parents assimilate information and react in a giant proportion of panic and hysteria. The second example comes from a very personal and dehumanizing experience that made her extremely vulnerable.

The experience has never been communicated on a public level, but it has been carried in her heart for seven years. It seems appropriate and timely to discuss it now, as it is a classic example of how an opportunist can use a very sensitive topic and manipulate it for his own advancement.

It has been chosen to be shared at this time because it will be very helpful in understanding how someone can hurt an innocent party for what he assumes would be logical reasoning in rendering him what he longs for, but cannot find honest methods for obtaining his desires or goals without earning the required credentials of honest labor.

The first example was when the author was a preschool teacher, and the media came out with reports that there were cases of child abuse in about three schools in California; two in the area where she lives. What happened was that a good case of paranoia developed with both the parents and staff.

Everyone went to work in a state of numbness. The parents became obsessed. Male members of the families of the staff couldn't be around the school at any time; even if they were dropping off or picking up the staff member at work. Heaven help us if the police were anywhere in sight, even though the school was located on a busy street, and they might be citing traffic violators. Teachers were afraid to give Johnny a hug or a tap on the shoulder for doing a great job. It was truly an insane situation, and why?

The public heard about three schools and were directing their opinion on every preschool due to the unfortunate situation of the three schools aired by the media. Worst of all, the owners of these schools were afraid of what the general public might think of their school. Mothers tried to show their knowledge when enrolling their offspring, but they were asking all the wrong questions and searching for the wrong objectives.

What happened in this scenario was that the general public was basing its opinions and concerns about all preschools on its limited knowledge of a few. Limited knowledge sometimes can be far worse than no knowledge at all. In forming an accurate assessment, parents should have some insight of human nature, averages, and general appearances.

Let's look at each of these for a moment. In interpersonal relationships, it's important to notice how the staff relates to the students and one another. Do they seem happy and effective in performing their job? Are they knowledgeable and skillful when they are interacting with the children? What knowledge have the parents accumulated? How many schools are there in the city? In the county? What is the success rate and the average length of attendance of the students?

Parents should be aware of what could happen, but base their opinions on the majority and not the minority. How is the school's general appearance? Is it neat and well organized? Being aware of what could happen is fine, as long as it doesn't immobilize a person into irrational thinking, fright, distrust, and not being able to assess situations correctly.

One of the major problems in the training of young children today is we are destroying their childhood and want them to grow up too quickly. One of the primary functions of a good preschool is helping the child to establish good social skills. Giving the child an awareness of life in general, in their preschool years is far more advantageous than a true academic program. If a child shows a natural inquisitiveness toward nature, numbers and words, the specifics will fall into line at the proper time. The child will have a broad base of assimilation, which will automatically encourage his creative or natural self.

While the first example had to do with mass hysteria on an issue, this second example is very personal and the sad experience which has to do solely with one man. Let me say that any person involved with abused children has the opportunity of an infraction being filed against him any time there is interaction. This type of child is very angry and generally disillusioned with life, which is a shame.

These young years, which should be the fun-filled and exciting years of a child's life, are burdened with a lifestyle beyond his years or experience. It's usually the child who files a report to his social worker. In this particular case, it was the owner of the youth home where my husband and I worked together who attempted to end my long tenure with children.

We had moved to a small city very close to the mountains. We got a job as youth counselors at a youth home, which was actually a beautiful ranch on thirteen acres of land. The children had the benefit of riding horses. When we got the job, we were not told that the ranch had been sold and our jobs would just be a temporary assignment. Naturally, being the last employees hired, we were the first to leave, with the rest eventually following.

The new administrator was going to open his own youth home, and we were very fortunate to be able to work for him (or so we thought at the time). He purchased one house and the arrangement was that my husband and I were to move in and be caretakers until it was ready for the residents. Well, it wasn't explained that my husband was to assist the carpenters in building another bedroom and bathroom. Next was the cyclone fence around the pool. Then it was painting the house on another piece of property that the owner had purchased as a rental.

Naturally, we weren't being paid. The owner did manage to take us to dinner a few times. He said that we would be paid as soon as he got some residents. The months went by, and no pay. Finally, after four months, he called us into the office, gave us a check for one month's salary, and said for us to take a few days off and when we returned, we would be managing another house that he purchased. The house was smaller, and that since I was getting older, I wouldn't have to work so hard. (Me, old, never -- at least as far as being active).

On the day before we were to return, we stopped by the house and learned that he had purchased two other houses. In the meantime, he was buying all this really expensive furniture, which certainly wasn't the type of decor that young people would enjoy.

One of the boys came running out to see me. This resident was released from the hospital psychiatric ward and into our care. He happened to be taking heavy medication so that he could function more effectively. I liked him. He was sweet, with blond hair and deep blue eyes. The boy came running to our car and said, "The owner said that you were fired for undressing in front of me the night I couldn't sleep and you slept in the game room fully dressed on the recliner chair. He made me say that you really did it and I know what happened, but he said he would beat me if I didn't say what he told me to say to Protective Services."

Well, we should have gotten smarter much sooner. How was the owner able to buy so many houses so fast and purchase all this expensive furniture? I believe he said that he had a good line of credit at one time when we were casually talking. Yet, remember he couldn't pay us for months. The real reason, we later learned, was that he certainly didn't have a cash flow; not even a trickle. He had the idea of letting us go because we were a couple and he had a single person that he could hire which, naturally, cut his payroll in half. He did hire a couple for another house, expected the husband to do all the work, and ended up not paying him either.

I spoke to one of the neighbors. She said that it was really a bad situation. Our replacement would have the bigger and older children beat up on the younger ones, so that it wouldn't be termed "abusive behavior", but just a fight between residents.

We moved to the next city and were soon to learn that the owner was called to the school. He went to pick a resident up and the child was crying and got underneath the desk. The owner tried calling him twice and when that didn't work, he proceeded to kick the boy extremely hard. The vice-principal saw the whole thing and when the owner returned home, the police came and handcuffed the owner and took him to jail.

In the meantime, my husband and I returned to the city and got another counseling job. We were there a week and were called to the main office. They did a reference check and the owner gave his story and blacklisted us. My new employer explained that he couldn't have us close to the children with that kind of report. He told us that he trusted us, but if Social Services heard what type of report the previous employer said, they might close his whole business down!

He asked us to do him a favor and work as managers for his pizza parlor, and he would attempt to get the matter cleared. We worked at the pizza parlor and it took over a year to clear the issue, even though Social Services said that they didn't have anything on us, but quite a bit on the owner!

For a person to do such a despicable thing to another individual is inhuman. You see, that's playing below the belt, so to speak, because it not only can ruin a person's reputation, but it eats away at one's very core.

Our cash resources were running extremely low. The arrangement was that we would get a reasonable salary and live in an apartment above the business. You should have seen this apartment. It was built in the early fifties, with metal cabinets, a living room, kitchen, a small bedroom that would only hold a full-sized bed, and one vanity. The bathroom was the best part of the apartment, as it was big with nice tile.

Across the hall from the apartment was the storage area for the businesses. While the apartment had central heating and air-conditioning, the thermostat was located in the outside hall, which was always cold, so once the temperature was set, it was always running and the apartment would become unbearably hot. Of course, then we would run out and shut it off, and later have to run out and turn it back on because then we were freezing.

To get to the apartment we had to climb up wooden stairs that were showing the bare wood. It was truly a "dream" place! Since a home is so very important to me, the first thing I did was cry and cry, and was wondering what in the world was happening to us. Shortly afterward, we decided to make the place as comfortable, attractive, and cozy as was humanly possible. We got some of our furniture out of storage, bought ceiling fans, mini blinds, and decorated in soft pastel colors.

It became transformed, and we ended up living in the apartment for over three years. It gave me a sense of contentment. The apartment became a sanctuary and an oasis against a troubled world. One good factor was that we were close to work, which this owner wanted, as the pizza parlor was opened twelve hours a day and six days a week.

We were working very hard and long hours, but it was fun and I can make a great pizza! We had regular customers and it was a very friendly and warm place. Everyone enjoyed one another, which helped divert my mind, as I was still attempting to cope with the problems of our association with the last employer.

When the employment with that youth home was terminated, we had filed for unemployment insurance to tide us over until we got work. We needed and received only one payment. It wasn't long before the drama started. We got a call from the insurance office that we were "given" a check and that it was ours, but we couldn't file for further benefits for five months if we needed to, because our former employer said that we were disqualified and that he was contemplating filing a suit against us for my so-called indecent exposure.

Now you would have to know something about me. You know the "perfect ten" figure? Well, my build is a far cry from it; maybe the "perfect twenty"! I think of myself as an extremely modest individual. I am not embarrassed with my physical body, but I certainly would never, ever, imagine myself indecently exposing my body.

The plot was thickening. I called the local unemployment office where we had originally filed our claim and the representative inquired, "What in the world is going on with this man? He says that he is a doctor with a Ph.D. and a Master's Degree in Social Work, but he is acting really weird. I checked and processed your claim and he had time to respond. After the time period elapsed, he calls and rambles on!"

We requested a hearing, which was conducted by a judge over the telephone since we had moved so far out of the area. It was a disaster, and due to his supposedly outstanding credentials, she ruled in the owner's favor.

Now my husband was starting to get agitated. He filed with the Labor Board for the back wages that we didn't receive. Again, because of his so-called credentials, the doctor won the judgment. "Fine," said my husband, "We'll take him to small claims court." Once again, the doctor won out.

Then, the doctor dropped a bombshell. He was counter-suing us for stealing food out of the house when we left! The truth of the matter is that we bought all the food and were feeding him! After all, I was preparing meals for us, and to be polite and gracious, he was always invited to eat with us. He never once purchased food for the house while we were there working before the residents arrived. In other words, he was suing us for taking our own food.

This was so ridiculous that even the judge was getting confused. He told us that he was setting another court date and for all of us to try and make some sense out of the charges. When we returned for the second court date, the owner wasn't present. The judge asked us if we would be willing to simply forget the charges as the plaintiff had called and said that it was impossible to appear, and, therefore, he was dropping the case! What happened?

Shortly after, we called the neighbor where we used to work. She said that we would be surprised at what was going on. She explained that a front page article appeared in the local newspaper and for me to send for some copies. Briefly, what follows is a summary of the article.

This man was buying the ranch that was sold where we first worked. He used someone else's fingerprints when he had to present them to the state for the youth homes. This news had appeared in a previous edition of the paper. It naturally triggered an investigation. It also triggered the memory in the mind of another resident in town about an article that appeared in *Newsweek* Magazine over ten years before this news story. This person thought that the owner was familiar for some strange reason. He thought that he might have read about him in a magazine. He decided to thumb through his collection and he found what he was looking to find.

This man found a 1978 article that described the method my ex-employer managed his career. These are the events of his "professional" life:

He graduated from a college in the Midwest with a Ph.D. He moved to California and settled with his family. He applied and got a position at a health care facility, producing the proper credentials, including a Master's Degree in social work. He was a good employee, but was not present at meetings when decisions had to be made on technical procedures for the care of the patients. After he was there several months, the state license inspectors were coming out to review the facility. This inspection would naturally include viewing employee records. Now, he was in a state of panic, as he was performing as a medical doctor, having only a Ph.D. He stole and took on the identity of a previous employee who was a qualified psychiatrist.

The psychiatrist had moved to another state. Since this man did not have all the needed papers or fingerprints, he took a trip to locate him. He confronted the psychiatrist, told him what he did, and that he needed some more material. Now, this psychiatrist thought the man was crazy, and naturally, refused such an unusual request. The man panicked and tried to kill the psychiatrist by strangulation. The psychiatrist called the police. There was another warrant out for him. The resident took this old article to the police and the rest is history!

After working in the pizza parlor, I was once again working in the youth homes. It wasn't long before we got a new resident that had stayed at the youth home from that beautiful small city. He told me that the owner was arrested, the business shut down, and the man was doing prison time.

If you are curious to know how he got his unlimited line of credit, he committed bigamy and used the woman's money and credit cards. She was trying to charge him and I don't know how the outcome of her association with him has been resolved.

Those are the specifics of the outward manifestation of the experience, but what it did to my being, emotions, and health is another story. In fact, it got so bad that I was ready to commit myself to a psychiatric hospital. I did make a quick visit, spent two hours, and returned home after the doctor prescribed Valium. It was really a mess. The Valium made me tired and sleepy, so I would drink tons of coffee, which then made me nervous. I was smart enough not to take more Valium, but not smart enough to keep away from aspirin.

Valium, coffee, and aspirin are not a good combination. I did have sense to stop, but in doing so, created a sensitivity and understanding that became too intense. I was also angry and emotionally distraught. I simply wanted to be left alone. I actually thought I was dying. I felt that I was all alone in the world. No one understood; only me.

My husband had lived through the experience too, but he wasn't the one that this man directed his actions toward. How could he possibly understand? I was putting him through his own emotional trauma by my own behavior. I couldn't eat, as food felt like a ton of bricks in my system. I couldn't go for a walk. I simply didn't have the strength. I would sit at the kitchen table and write and doodle for hours. I didn't want to get dressed, because I certainly wasn't going anywhere. Why fix my hair? I still wasn't going anywhere. I would fall asleep because I was so depressed, and then wake up in the middle of the night and pace the floor for hours and drink coffee. Hour upon hour, night after night.

The doctor couldn't help me. I wouldn't listen. His solutions sounded silly to me. Why try to get on with my life, when the years I devoted to children, my life's purpose, were over? Why pretend? Why try? What was the reason to try?

My anger really flared up when I thought about this poor boy who loved me and was put in the situation that he had to lie, knew that he was doing it, didn't want to do it, but knew he had to do it for his own safety. He also was a very brave child, because I knew that he was quite aware that the odds were, because of the conditions, he would be returned to the hospital.

He was a very sweet child, and when he told me, he put his arms around my neck and asked me if I was mad at him. How could I be mad at a child who displayed so much love and caring that he had to tell me what was happening? I think about him often and hope that he is all right. I know in my heart that he is, because in his own delicate way, he is smart, and more importantly, he is a survivor.

My physical body was beginning to feel my pain. I had sinus headaches. My ears hurt. I had cramps in my stomach. My legs ached, and my broken foot hadn't healed. Finally, my immune system began to break down. At last, it spoke to me. "Sweetheart," it said, "You are giving me too much to fight. I am trying but I need your help. You haven't been doing your part. You haven't been eating or sleeping; and that mixture of coffee, Valium and aspirin isn't helping. However, the worst part is your intuitive self. You know that all these things that you are doing and thinking about aren't real. In worldly terms, you can't fight anything that isn't real, because not being real, there is nothing to fight. However, you are real."

"Stop what you are doing because that isn't real either. Help me to help you. Right now, I am fighting too many battles. First, it's your stomach, then your head, legs, and foot. I am fighting too many battles without any ammunition. Please nourish your body and mind. Help yourself to help me."

Michael Jackson believes that children are innocent little human beings. After grieving and thinking about this child, he taught me a lesson. The child knew in his heart what the events of that evening were. He also knew that this man could physically inflict pain. He knew that he had to protect himself, but at the very same time, he knew that he had to protect me by advising me of what transpired.

He did this still having the insight that he could not trust the owner, and that although he agreed with the person, since the man couldn't be trusted, his own future was in question. He understood perfectly that surviving this one encounter was just the beginning of what was to follow. He also took a calculated risk of being caught talking with me. If he was seen by the owner or another child, further punishment would surely follow.

The master will always be willing to take a stand for his beliefs. He will listen to the calling of the heart even at the cost of the outcome. The loyalty to the self is far more important than the pain and ridicule of the populace.

I don't know how long the depression lasted. At the time, it seemed like forever. I don't know when it happened, but one day, I did realize that I couldn't handle it any more by myself. This young boy helped me. He was brave. He was strong. He was going to keep on going and beat the odds. If a young child can do it, why can't I? I thought of him being alone in strange surroundings. Believe you are okay; embrace it.

There is a Higher Source in life working, and part of that Source was in me. The minute I reached a decision to let go of the problem, I was fine. It's seven years later, and I know that the Source is still with me and will always give me the characteristics of intuition, inspiration, and thought. These are my guidelines. They are an inherent part of my being. They are my comfort and my salvation against a troubled world. They create both the peace and the spark that give me my own empowerment.

Photo Courtesy of MJJ Productions

Looking back, much was benefited from the experience. It gave me a greater sense of purpose and direction. It taught me what is important and necessary in life, and to cut through the trivial stuff that people think and do. Now I concentrate on what really counts in life; what I know and think about myself.

It's strange because when something that we envision is disastrous in the physical world, our energy is directed in that specific area. We don't realize that the outward reflection of ourselves is the total mirroring of our inner self. The two words used to describe this are character and reputation. The latter can't change unless the former is transformed, which rarely happens.

The masters know this principle well. They understand that our character is basic to who we are and reflects in our manifestations and our personality in the form of our reputation. It is a puzzlement when someone in the limelight has undue criticism levied upon them. The first question people ask is, "What is this going to do to his reputation?" They imagine careers going down the drain.

Of course, if there is a character flaw, the chances are that it is more than likely to happen. The flaw, however, was always present in their character before the criticism, and was just waiting for the opportunity to present itself. If a person exhibits a good, strong character throughout his life, and it is consistent, it would be very unlikely that it would change because that's a person's code of ethics in which he produces and operates in the world.

What was the reason in telling my own encounter in a book about a master? It seemed fitting, and the timing seemed to be right. We have to relax and not be so quick to form judgments. We must remember to observe, listen, and analyze with the purpose to understand the truth, and not join in with those who think that the best way to get ahead is to destroy, or put another person down, to gain what they desire in life.

Chapter 8:

The Master Applies Wisdom in Solving Issues

"Ours is a world of nuclear giants and ethical infants.
We know more about killing than we do about living."
- General Omar Bradley

"To me, true bravery is settling differences without a fight and having the
wisdom to make that solution possible."
- Michael Jackson

Our courts have lawyers to defend their clients. However, recently it seems like some of these lawyers are more interested in enhancing their own reputations, instead of sincerely defending their clients. The courts are not the arena for theatrics.

All government agencies are established for the betterment of the citizens. Their purpose isn't to exert power, and it is not about factions, one group against another. The solution is oneness; all of us working peacefully together to bring the people who have committed a crime to justice. We must have clarity and purpose in expanding and innovating better methods of doing things.

The populace sits in judgment of others of equal kind. Many times throughout the book, we discuss the advancement we have attained in the field of technology. Yet, in bringing harmony to the planet, we still use the very same methods of rehabilitation. Here we are using the bandaid mentality.

Let's review how a master creates. He starts with a creative idea. It's just an idea; nothing physical at the moment. In order to develop a song, dance, painting, book, lecture, or philosophy, he has to visualize the desired outcome, and commence through the various stages to arrive at the desired result. He starts within himself and works outward; a bandaid starts from the outside.

Healing always commences at the source of the wound. We are quick to identify the problems when they are brought to our attention. Then we run out and try to scout the offenders and hand out some form of punishment. The type of punishment is the same type that has been used since the beginning of time: Catch them, give them a trial, and incarcerate them, possibly for life, or even the death penalty. This is not the solution as we have more of the same problem.

Human life is a gift of nature and should not be tampered with by anyone. Families who have lost a person because of the senseless act of another should have the comfort of knowing that the offender has been dealt with in a comparable manner. However, there is no punishment that is going to equate the loss of another person's life.

The problem never stops. We give life sentences or the death penalty and yet there are still murders. We imprison drunk drivers and they are still driving on our highways. We are concerned about the spread of sexual diseases and now we have a sexual epidemic. We have more young girls of high school age having babies and on welfare. Lately, we are on sex offenders, but sexual abuse is still going on.

We have senate hearings to attempt to get the most qualified representatives, and yet the media is reporting scandals in government from the national to the local levels. We are spending more money in the military operations to foreign countries and they are still troubled. What is going wrong? We attempt to advise other countries on what they are doing that is not right, yet, we arguing among ourselves about the personal and private characteristics of our leaders, which are really trivial when it comes to running the country.

Answers! Answers! Where are the solutions? Masters! Help! What would they advise us? Well, Michael gives us his beliefs:

> "The lyrics of *Beat It* express something I would do if I were in trouble. Its message -- that we should abhor violence -- is something I believe deeply... If you fight and get killed, you've gained nothing and lost everything. You're the loser, and so are the people who love you."[43]

Michael also mentioned that revenge is alien to him. If violence and revenge are not the proper solutions, what are? The answer is in education and knowledge, combined with the creative process. Michael explains another helpful component:

> "To me, true bravery is settling differences without a fight and having the wisdom to make that solution possible."[44]

The media has been reporting stories of random shootings, and killings of several innocent people who fell prey to the action of a single gunman. At first, such reports were few and far between; now they seem to be a common occurrence. We learn of them taking place in subways, in the government, and in private businesses. Even children are finding or purchasing weapons and by accident are killing a family member or friend.

We ask ourselves why such severe incidents could ever happen. After an investigation, the reason surfaces. Its cause could be a political belief, a distressed marriage, a lost love affair, a financial gain, a bitter employee or loss of employment, a terminal illness, or a curious child. When we know the reason, do we really know the truth? A master knows that the difficulty lies before the manifestation of a physical act. In his search for truth, he looks for the underlying cause so that the repetitive behavior will cease and the world can be healed.

In all of the cases, the truth is found by integration of a child's environment during the formative years of his development. Youthful people become adults. Adults learn from their experience, education, training, and most importantly, from example.

The state of Florida has been plagued with senseless crimes of murder, and many more criminal acts, done by juveniles. Many of the victims are tourists from other countries. Florida believes in incarcerating the youth for the purpose of training. The reason for this method is obvious and twofold: (1) To get offenders temporarily out of the mainstream of society; and (2) To correct the deviant behavior.

California has implemented the "Three strikes, you're out" law. This means if a resident is convicted of three felonies, he automatically goes to prison. This may not be as good as it seems. While it may keep offenders from reappearing on our streets, it will affect the state's economy because the law does not take into consideration the degree of the felony. It might leave a huge debt for the next generation, who had nothing to do with the problem.

The two states are attempting to solve the issue of eliminating crime but their solutions are in direct contrast. California has said that it has incarcerated the offenders but that they return to society and repeat the same behavior, and that, therefore, Florida's theory wouldn't work in California. Why is this?

The answer is that neither system will be a satisfactory solution in reducing crime itself unless each state gets at the cause of why the offender chose the deviant action to meet his needs. Was the action due to faulty physical or faulty psychological thought processes? In either case, society has to take a shared responsibility. So that we can take full responsibility in solving the determining factor for the restitution of an individual, it is necessary, first and foremost, to get at the internal causes.

The cause of deviant behavior can be physiological. We know that our body is a very complex creation. If one aspect is not working properly and is not sending the appropriate message to the brain, there can be disastrous results. This is due primarily to a chemical imbalance somewhere within the body.

The cause of deviant behavior can also be psychological. To correct the problem, it is necessary to understand human nature and the learning process. All actions that we exhibit are based on what we know. What our understanding is based upon is what we are taught, and thereby experience.

While we may be able to see and know what is right, if we have not been educated in the proper means of fulfilling what is considered prudent, we do not know how to use our empowerment to execute those needs. We, in turn, look for examples or role models. In the case of the criminal, the wrong example is chosen, because he has not experienced the proper training of using the positive thought process.

We see this when family histories are studied. In many cases, the same deviant patterns of behavior keep on repeating in each generation. The reason for this is that the cycle isn't broken because the cause for the behavior isn't determined, and the family doesn't have correct and positive role models to serve as an example for the proper behavior to emulate.

Earlier it was mentioned that one thought has the power to change the destiny of mankind. While California and Florida each have some validity to their respective theories, we can also see their shortcomings. What would happen if we were to use the creative source and combine the best ideas from both of them?

Perhaps California should be concerned with correcting the first offense, not by imprisonment, but by getting that person the correct training, making sure that it is comprehensive in getting at the internal cause of the deviant behavior. If the training Florida uses does not get at the internal cause, and does not change the thought process of the offender, his behavior will be repetitive.

As with everything, the true solution is in networking by the states to develop and expand knowledge. When it comes to the life of another individual, there is no room for a mistake. In making one, we are then as guilty as the person who committed the crime. Therefore, one of the best solutions might be to have a board with representatives from all the states, taking the best ideas from each of them.

Rehabilitation should be the key for minor offenders, and that way people can continue to make a contribution to society. The cause for the action should be discovered and the individual should be taught to see where he went wrong. If the cause isn't determined, the acts or conditions will keep perpetuating. It is simply deciding how we intend to spend our money: On incarceration, or rehabilitation.

This chapter does not represent whether the present types of punishment should be abolished or even changed. The point is that such punishment should be the right and just prescription for the individual whose fate is determined by our judicial system.

As with every decision in life, it has to be made on facts, and not interpretation, opinion, or feelings. This is very difficult to do because all of us base our viewpoints on our experiences. In the case of determining justice, we have to project how we would feel if we were both the accused and the victim. While emotions run high for both parties, this cannot be the determining factor. We would need to know that every conceivable fact was uncovered. Remember, no one can arrive at an honest opinion unless all of the facts are at his disposal. The most important factor that must be ascertained is why the individual performed the act, and if he is of sound body and mind.

Naturally, the prominent enactment of the crime is clear. What isn't always clear is why it was done. If we don't know the reason, we don't know whether it will be repeated and if proper treatment will ensure that the person will not be a continued threat to the survival of innocent people.

We have two distinct factions at work in the courtroom. There are lawyers who see their position in its entirety. Those representing the defendant understand that the people of the state want justice done. How is this accomplished? We know that if we understand the actions of a person, we then know something about that individual. We believe that in a criminal charge the people of the state feel that the actions of the defendant are against the governing laws. It is up to the prosecution to produce the evidence to substantiate the claims.

One of the phases of the judicial system that needs to be given careful analyzing is in the selection of a competent jury. In looking at the purpose and manner from the master's point of view, several factors need to be taken under consideration, and he must look at the scope of the task in front of him.

First and foremost, he is concerned with the value of life. If he were to find it necessary to sit in judgment of another sister or brother, he would demonstrate the same care that he takes in the development of the manifestation of his talent. He would study about the judicial systems of the past and the present. He would be quick to notice that it has not advanced to the present accomplishments and thinking process of modern times.

He solves such questions through applying intuition, inspiration, and thought. He would enlist the most qualified people for the jury who are going to determine the fate of the defendant. He wouldn't want people to serve who are not qualified.

Using the creative process, we could ask, what would happen if both parties worked as a unit to attempt to discover the reasons behind the action? What would happen if both sides worked hand-in-hand as one team with different views? What would happen if all the evidence was gathered and presented as a joint effort with each side giving their interpretation? What would happen if both sides wanted to see the same conclusion but presented different reasons for arriving at the verdict? If the evidence isn't clear and factual, and there is use of projection, would a guilty verdict be given?

In truth, there couldn't be such a verdict, and unless new factual information was presented, there would be no reason for an appeal or mistrial, and possibly millions of dollars would be saved. If we, once again, use the teachings of the master and discover how he applies his knowledge in the creation of this talent, we would elaborate on our own thinking process.

Photo Courtesy of MJJ Productions

Michael Jackson's contribution starts with the development of his talent, and the results of his manifestation transcend to different areas of his life, in turn bettering mankind and the planet. By using his talent, he became aware of the need for the advancement of the thinking process of the general population. He gave us examples by observing his gifts to the planet in the form of his humanitarian efforts. At the same time, the universe, being receptive to his offerings, has enhanced his own life, his individual lifestyle, and increased his monetary rewards beyond measure. It is important to realize that the desire to share his talent with the world came first, then came his personal material benefits.

Applying this very same creative process, we would understand that we must develop our own resources before we can enjoy the treasures of gifts of the planet. One of the first places to begin is in our interactions and the forming of judgments of our fellow man.

One of the most obvious uses of making judgments falls on our judicial system. The final judgment when using this system is in the hands of the jury. In society's earnest desire to see that the defendant receives a fair trial, the jury is chosen from the mainstream of the citizens. Using the creative process of the master, let us imagine how this could be more accurate in meeting the judgment of the defendant.

We already discovered that the master networks with the best people who can fulfill his needs in enhancing his primary idea. He is looking for individuals who are knowledgeable in his specific endeavor. He is also aware that the population is limitless for securing talent. He is searching for the best people who can use their expertise to meet his goal. He narrows his selection to the most qualified individuals.

At the same time, he is very much aware of what he doesn't know. In the selection of a competent jury to sit in judgment of one of our own, the same technique should be applied, as the future of the person standing on trial will be radically changed.

Using myself as an example, it is apparent what type of trial would be suitable for me to serve on as a juror. My field of expertise is with the family and children. It becomes quickly apparent what type of trial would be out of my scope of service. I am not an accountant. I am not a computer whiz. Since I have a very strong appreciation of life, I would be incapable of making a decision on taking another person's life. It is totally foreign to my comprehension for anyone to conceive of performing such an act, and yet I would not feel that I could ever imagine giving anyone the death sentence. In my mind, such a decision is left up to a much Higher Source than myself.

If by such a chance I were to have someone sit in judgment of my life, I would want the most qualified people on the jury. It would also become apparent to me rather quickly that the modern methods of specialization are not always applied in the selection of the jury. The same old methods have been applied for centuries. The selection of the jury would have to be updated to meet the knowledge and understanding of specialization of our generation.

The thought would come to me by intuition that, if I were to have a fair and honest decision made on the future of my life, it would be necessary to have the most competent panel; not just as witnesses, because serving in that capacity they are not required to make a judgment call.

If it were on a murder charge, the best psychiatrists, psychologists, investigators, and criminalists would be the type of individuals I would hope to be on my jury. If it were other charges, the same rationale would be applied. If it were embezzlement, a team of highly respected accountants would suffice. If it were computer fraud, people who were accomplished in their comprehension of computer technology would serve nicely.

We might ask ourselves how the selection of such specialized persons could be accomplished. One way might be the legal team's knowledge of securing such people. Another might be as simple as each time we register and fill out the form, there are questions as to our vocation and talents.

In using this type of method, it could be seen as giving too much consideration to the defendant. If we expand our thinking process and let it reach out to others, we have advanced civilization. Insofar as thinking on the realm of the master, we free ourselves of the possibility of making false judgments and know in our hearts, to the best of our ability, the decision is made on fact, rather than opinion.

The master wants unity in the world. The world is all inclusive in all aspects of life. If the planet is to operate on a belief of oneness, it has to operate as a unit in all areas.

In this century, we see and understand the importance of teamwork and networking. If we are going to get the true significance, it must apply anytime we interact with another individual in meeting a specific goal. To do otherwise, we are not displaying a unified world, but one of division. We are not experiencing the fullness and abundance of life. We are operating on a sense of limitation.

Many of the populace would respond by remarking that this is the way things are done, and that one person's idea cannot change the world. If we look at the accomplishments of people who have changed the destiny of mankind by a new invention, or in the field of medicine by discovering a cure for disease, we know that this isn't true. Such individuals used their intuitive source, their creative process, for unleashing their idea to advance the previous thought process of man.

One of the major diseases plaguing this generation is AIDS. Michael Jackson has taken a particular interest in this deadly disease, along with many other members of the entertainment industry, including Elizabeth Taylor. We have mentioned the need for parents to educate their children on the subject. The author believes it cannot be done simply in a discussion or two. Education begins when the child is very young, on the proper respect for his own perfect gift from creation.

The child has to be taught the primary purpose of sex. The continued survival of any species is dependent upon creating new members for each group of inhabitants. The author remembers taking six of the boys of the youth home to a fast food restaurant for lunch. One of the boys mentioned something about another boy's girlfriend. We somehow got into the subject of sex.

This was an opportunity for me to listen. The boys believed that most sixteen year olds were sexually active. It was explained that the primary function of sex was procreation. Of course, they laughed. They were asked if they were ready to be a father. They chuckled some more. They said that it was kind of a status thing. The advice they were given was, "Don't try to outsmart nature."

If something wasn't enjoyable, did they think that many people would participate in the activity? Their response was a loud "No". They did agree on something: That nature knows about us. If sex wasn't enjoyable, the species' duration couldn't be guaranteed. Man loves to do things that are enjoyable. Since sex is enjoyable, he has to have a reason that is logical so that he can participate in such a pleasurable activity. Man establishes a code that makes it totally acceptable. He says it's all right if you are married or are deeply in love with another person. Society also establishes that if a child is born, it must be properly cared for in receiving his basic needs.

The boys were asked if they believe doing something secretive from their parents makes it okay. We talked about being young and that it was for a short period of a lifetime; adulthood lasts for the rest of a person's life. They were told that most men reach their potential in their careers when they are in their early forties. They were asked if they knew the correct reason for this. Of course, they shook their heads. It was mentioned that these men use more of their energy in their jobs. It was explained that the boys' increased energy, due to their increased hormones, can be diverted to sports or reflect on expanding their talent.

When we tell youth to practice "safe sex", we are giving them a double message, and showing them that we don't believe in our hearts what we are telling them. We are also displaying a lack of confidence and trust. In essence, we are saying, "We are telling you this, but we don't trust you. We don't believe that you will follow the advice we are giving you, therefore, practice "safe sex" ". This is so strange because we don't instruct them about other ways that might be injurious to their well being in the same manner.

The other reason is the response to our own thinking process on a particular subject. In the discussion of this sensitive topic the ease in which it is handled will illustrate to the receiver our willingness and naturalness by the approach that is applied. The listener is quick in interpreting the lack of confidence or insecurity of the speaker. It is important to remember that what we are looking for, we will find. If we believe that the method nature uses to propagate the planet is beautiful and natural, it will reflect in the sincerity of the delivery. On the other hand, if we view it as something secretive and wrong, this too will be disclosed.

There is an interesting ending to this conversation. When we got up to leave the table, a young woman with two children smiled and told us that she overheard the discussion. She remarked that she was going to remember the approach and use the same method when the need became apparent with her children. She couldn't get over the ease and naturalness the subject was given. In keeping in mind the teaching of the master in presenting a topic of discussion, she was advised to take advantage of the opportunity by taking her clue from the children and letting them serve as her guide in giving and receiving information.

Another reason adolescents might vie for "safe sex" is that, as caretakers, we don't handle our own lives in the same manner we want children to do and, hence, lack credibility. A master always sets the correct example, otherwise he won't have a receptive audience.

The use of drugs is another crisis in our society. A master knows that the usage of anything foreign to the body is giving the person a false sense of himself. The decade of the nineties is full of stress. People who take drugs of any form are using the bandaid mentality. They are attempting to use an outside remedy to an internal problem. The use of such a substance is camouflaging both the source of the feelings and the body's natural healing process. It makes a person less diligent in his actions and response to them.

One dominant factor is the carelessness in the handling of the drug, and its application to the body. This has far reaching complications, not only as a contributing factor to AIDS, but to one's very life. We have to be ready and willing to experience anything that comes into our lives and find that balance that is normal and natural remedies to our inherent feelings. Those feelings are nature's way of a warning that something isn't just right with our being.

The solution is examining our inner self in locating the cause. It might tell us to slow down, have better self-esteem, get more knowledge, use good self talk concerning our predicament, or seek out a reliable source to guide us.

We think we are somehow helping to solve the issues of society by forming judgments based upon what information we are receiving. This is not accurate and could be damaging to the person or situation. It has already been stated how Michael feels about judging anyone unless you have spoken to the person. The problem is that many of the people that we learn about, we cannot talk to personally. What should we do then? We have to have some kind of a guideline. If the situation or person's behavior is in direct contrast to what we knew of previous conditions, it probably is false. However, there is always the first time. In this case, we have to form an opinion on what we do know. Since we don't know anything for sure, we cannot judge. We can't know what we don't experience. We just have to wait and see.

The use of projection is very misleading. We think if conditions are a certain way, the situation must conform to what may or usually transpires. This can't be further from the truth; in fact, it may be in direct contrast. People like to judge others, but would not like to be judged with the same yardstick. This happened a lot with people who are in the limelight because they are most familiar to us and more visible.

In order to have credibility with other nations, we have to support our government. If we cannot support the people we have in office, how are foreign countries going to respect them? We are a democratic country and we have elections. We also have the privilege of recall, or even impeachment.

We must also understand that the government and law enforcement agencies are under the direction of "We the People", and they should follow our directives. They, however, cannot do this unless we inform them of our wishes and how we expect them to interact. Sometimes, they too need to be reminded that their job is one of service and not power. The former is positive and the latter, a negative form of fulfilling their duties.

Some of the issues that are presently confronting our society have been mentioned, and now it should be realized some of the opinions that we have in our minds are not always the most prudent way in arriving at a solution. You see, in many cases, we are conditioned to think by the sources from which we are receiving our information. In a very real sense, we are brainwashed to respond in a certain manner by the media. Remember, it was mentioned that the media is in business to create and maintain a market. Through various methods, they have it down to a science what the general public wants to know, so that it will listen to their broadcast and they will maintain their ratings, or the customers will continue to purchase their publications.

If we were to describe the age the media is in, it could very well be classified as being in the age of "criticism and attack" on individuals in the spectrum, ranging from the government to the entertainment industry, which in recent years has been one of the hardest fields under scrutiny.

When Michael Jackson gave his opinion in answering questions from the press, he felt to answer their questions about untrue statements could create another story and establish more and more statements that would need explanation. A master knows when it is beneficial to remain silent, because he knows, by not having additional information, the subject will experience a slow death.

There needs to be more discernment in evaluating what we see, hear and read. The reliability of the source of gathering of information is crucial if we are to get an accurate assessment. As it was previously mentioned, the true characteristic of a highly intelligent person is to be keenly aware of what he doesn't know. Unless we have all the facts before us, we know nothing!

This is a major flaw presently in our judicial system, as it is relying heavily on circumstantial evidence. This means if there is evidence, or if witnesses can testify that they have seen the crime and believe that they are giving an accurate assessment of what has happened, the jury will no doubt weigh the evidence and testimony and render a judgment.

Now this sounds logical and fair, but is it? Well, while Michael enjoys watching cartoons, the author enjoys watching Court TV. One instance stands out in her mind. There was a panel of legal experts discussing the difficult time the jury could have in reaching a verdict. Right in the middle of their discussion, a television technician came up and told the commentator his microphone wasn't working properly. He fixed the commentator's microphone on the lapel of his suit.

In the meantime, a lady snuck up on the left-hand side of the screen. She quickly disappeared. The commentator quickly discovered that his coffee mug was missing. They determined that this lady must have taken the cup. There was a line-up of possible suspects. The panel made a calculated guess. Well, none of the three ladies in the line-up was the culprit. None of the legal experts could observe everything and recall exactly what happened when they were even witnessing the whole action.

Circumstantial evidence is difficult to ascertain because, once again, it uses projection. If there is this evidence belonging to a defendant, then certainly he must be guilty. Right? Well? Do we really know for sure? Honestly, without a question of a doubt?

The best action is for everyone not to express an opinion until the truth becomes available. The real truth may never surface. Then what is a person to do? The answer is to rely on a reliable source, which might be the person or your own self, and remain neutral.

A major problem in finding the remedy to issues is there are many opportunists in the world who will use and twist the system for their own benefit and gain. This type of individual wants the enumeration based on someone else's labor. Michael's viewpoint on revenge can apply here. The universe somehow equals the scale because the rewards never last, or do all they could have by being acknowledged through sincere effort. The person who gives the penitence receives more abundance of value in the same token.

All of us do not see the seriousness of accusing a party of a crime and the manner in which the defendant is treated. If we are to follow the Constitution, we are to work on the premise that each individual is innocent until he is proven guilty. This infers that a person who has not been proven of the enactment of the crime is considered by the people as innocent of the crime.

Looking at the manner in which we form opinions and the fulfillment of suitable restitution, we are, in many cases, working backward. We appear to be more interested in finding a person and dealing out a punishment than we are at getting at the cause. While bringing an offender to justice is noble, what happens if we make a horrendous mistake? If this person is still alive, we allow him to go free. We have not equaled the score for the discomfort, the pain, nor the humiliation that he had to endure.

We do the same thing in war. If the ruling party is causing us pain, we take the military, the airplanes, the ammunition, and try to convince the country to conform. The cause is usually the governing party and not the citizens who reside under their domain. In doing this, we haven't dealt with the cause and have put many innocent people to an untimely death.

Every one of us can see violence and crime from our businesses, to our schools, our streets, and our homes. How did it all start? It started with using the wrong examples. We might be raising a generation of insensitive people. If we are using weapons, force, and power as quick remedies to problems, that is what many youth are absorbing as solutions. This usually happens when their concerns haven't been heard.

What do the masters tell us? Michael Jackson believes that applying wisdom, and not violence, is the method to be used if we are going to heal the world. Masters always search for peaceful means to settle the wounds of mankind. A question that we must keep asking ourselves is, "Is this solution the best for all concerned, and the advancement of mankind?". In responding to the question by imploring wisdom, we become part of the solution and not the problem.

There are many people of the world who need our help and assistance, both at home and abroad. The answer is in good communication and education along with lending a helping hand. The truth of the matter is that we have to truly understand ourselves before we can understand another country or individual. This takes work in expanding our own knowledge and viewpoints. It is also admitting our own weaknesses and shortcomings.

We tend to think that one person does not have the ability or resources to change the world. As such, we do not see our own true worth and position which we hold. Remember earlier in the book, it was mentioned that a person tells himself that he cannot act on intuition? The master's reply was, "And why not?".

A master does not think along the lines of limitation and arbitrary boundaries. The real truth of the matter is that a person is as important, intelligent, and creative as he believes himself to be. Michael never thought that his talent or creativity was limited. He would watch and read about his mentors and past masters. This not only added to his knowledge but instilled within him that if they became proficient and used their talent to the highest degree, there was no reason that he couldn't do likewise.

Michael Jackson also learned to rely on his intuitive source and talent. He didn't question it. This is the way mankind advances. It takes an idea, expands upon it, and elevates it to the next level. One simple idea with networking with others had already changed the destiny of mankind on numerous subjects and accomplishments from the arts to the sciences. It starts with a basic question, "Is there a better, more efficient, or more creative way?".

A master lives his life according to his understanding and sets the right example by practicing what he presents to the audience in the form of a message. While Michael Jackson performs, or speaks at various events, he gives his public the proper example. He tells us that children are innocent.

Photo Courtesy of MJJ Productions

If children are innocent, why do we have so much violence when they become adults? The answer is that they are internalizing the wrong examples. It was mentioned earlier that Michael believes the solution to violence is in using wisdom. Adults' first duty is to set the proper example. Our first introduction to the world is by what we see and hear. What a child first views and listens to should take place in a nurturing environment. If such an atmosphere isn't present in the familiar surroundings of the home, the child looks elsewhere for role models and acceptance.

If an adult hasn't had such guidance and training when he was young, it infiltrates in every aspect of his grown up life, not only in his personal experiences, but with others in the workplace and society as a whole. Societies are communities that become states, which then expand to nations. Since, in all practicality, adults cannot return to their younger years, a master fully realizes he has to go back and pick up the missing stages of his childhood in order to have complete knowledge and mastery of life's principles.

In solving such issues of crime and violence, we must once again turn to the teachings of the masters. We don't know what the master's opinion or solution might be on a particular issue. We should not attempt to enter into his private thoughts, as in truth, unless we had an audience before him, we wouldn't know what his thoughts would be.

In the quest for possible options, information would have to be assimilated in regard to what has been previously manifested or said publicly. Let's examine what we do know. Michael Jackson is keenly aware that the solution to the wounds of the world commences with healing. When we are hurt physically or emotionally, healing is a peaceful remedy for our pain.

In studying the master, he looks at the scope and ramifications of the subject, whether it be in association with his craft, or an issue in its entirety. He has to ascertain the results of his actions and compare them with his immediate and long term goals. It may start by asking himself a simple question such as, "Where do I go from here?"

In reading the previous chapters, we know that revenge in the form of making someone pay for something that they have done is alien to Michael Jackson. We also know that he asks himself what actions of the present affect the past. We know that he believes that violence is not the proper solution in solving problems, and that the loss of a loved one has consequences for many persons other than the victim. He views wisdom as the trait to employ in finding and experiencing healing.

When a defendant is being charged for a hideous crime and is facing a long prison sentence or the death penalty, we have to ask ourselves if that is really what we want. Once again, we have to consider Michael's wisdom when he responded, "I don't know anything for sure. I am still learning."

In essence, we are making life-long and life-threatening decisions without knowing everything. Unless we have all the facts, are knowledgeable, and have the ability to assimilate information correctly, we cannot make an accurate appraisal.

Our judicial system has been basically operating in the same manner for centuries. While there have been some revisions, the primary format has been the same. Therefore, it has not taken into consideration the advancement of and understanding that has been learned about human nature. One might reply that the system has served us well. Another person might see a need to expand and update it to correspond with modern times.

The master is aware that the world operates on a sense of balance. In finding the correct solution, we have to balance the scale between the defendant and his crime. It was mentioned earlier that in order to heal a wound, we have to look underneath the bandaid at the internal cause. In concerning ourselves with the crime, we have to learn the cause, and our assessment of that cause has to be accurate. It applies to the universal law of cause and effect.

Let's explore with our intuitive resource exactly what happens when we give another human a lifetime prison sentence from the perspective of "We The People". Society has already lost. By putting an individual in prison, we have also given the community the sentence of supporting that individual for the prescribed duration. We have put an additional tax burden on a troubled economy. We are making the defendant less self efficient while all of us are scrambling around working honestly to make ends meet and give a large portion of our income to support our country. While, in a sense, the prisoner has lost his freedom of choice, he has gained extreme freedom in not having to concern himself with the costs of personal maintenance. He may have a prison job to perform but he knows that he will have a roof over his head, clothes on his back, and food to eat. These are things that we have to work very diligently for our welfare and survival.

Prison has a definite purpose of protecting society by incarcerating persons who are a threat to its survival. In keeping our thoughts along the lines of the masters, we take the thinking process to the next level by asking, "Who is a permanent threat to us?"

Most crimes are done for personal or financial gain in various forms and degrees. The degree is the key in finding the solution. If a person wasn't a continued threat, what would happen if, using the creative process, we responded, "We are going to make you do retribution in direct balance to your crime. We are expanding our work program. You will enhance our country by being the ones who plant our crops, work in our hospitals, work in the field of social services, build our bridges, and you must find such a job and turn over half of your earnings to feed the hungry, build homes for the homeless, provide government service, and develop your talents to serve others. We are teaching a lesson that you need to learn the most; there is no easy way to success. By our choice, and not yours, you will devote the rest of your life and talent to the betterment of mankind. There is no quick way to financial security without honest labor. You will now learn the hard way to success. However, we will also show you the joy of honesty and integrity."

In trying to attempt to resolve a problem, a master must look for the possible cause. He then, by applying his knowledge and education, applies his wisdom. In using an example, let us take the highest position of our country. In searching for a solution, we have to be aware of what we do know in finding the answer to the unknown. All of us can remember our first civic class; it took place when we were about in the eighth grade.

We learned very quickly of the greatness of our forefathers and the use of their knowledge and creative source. In establishing the Constitution, they foresaw in their minds the future of their country. This document has served us well for over two hundred years. This is an amazing accomplishment.

Remember the Preamble? We had to memorize it, and the author can remember it clearly and recite it to this day. It is a beautiful document in its simplicity:

> "We the people of the United States, in order to form a more perfect Union, establish justice, insure domestic tranquillity, provide for the common defense, promote the general welfare, and secure the blessings of liberty to ourselves and our prosperity, do ordain and establish this Constitution for the United States of America."

Perhaps, in all honesty, if we really take a good look at our lives, our desires, and our hopes, and balance them with our thoughts, actions, and the intuitive and creative sources that reside within us, we are the responsible ones for not making our lives and the planet into the beautiful and harmonious place the universe has envisioned for us. We have to take total responsibility for our opinions, actions, and the results that occur from them.

It has always been interesting for the author to listen to the opinions of others when they express themselves on a particular issue. It's interesting because most of our opinions do not take into consideration the larger scope of the manifestations of what those thoughts might encompass.

After reading to this place in the book, it has become apparent that we should develop the skills of the master in forming an accurate opinion. How would a person of Michael Jackson's stature conjecture?

We are not searching for his viewpoint because, naturally, this is not the object of our intentions. Our purpose is to determine how a master might arrive at a conclusion. A master uses what he does know as a base of conclusion. A master uses what he does know as a base of exploring the unknown. He is aware that the president is the highest representative and statesman for our country. He symbolizes the needs and wishes of the citizens. He has been elected to serve in that capacity by the majority of the people of the country.

A master knows when to take responsibility and will not evade his duty and his appreciation for the priviledge of living and benefiting from all of the services that our nation provides, including his freedom to expand and manifest his talent to his full potential.

A master always studies the past masters as his guide in forming an assessment of his viewpoints on a present condition or accomplishment. He readily comprehends what the forefathers foresaw for the history of their country. By careful observation of the constituents of life, liberty, and pursuit of happiness, there is a constant balance, just as there is in the universe.

In the formation of the government, and its three segments, the wishes, goals, and desires of the general population are assured. A master believes in expansion and sees that the officials of our government are only the beginning of the democratic process. At any period, the people have options to express their needs to that governing body. It is the responsibility of the people to inform their representatives of their opinion. Each representative and senator has an office that is open to telephone calls and letters.

If the subject is taken full circle, once again, the plight of the country, state or county rests on the individual. Before any citizen should give an opinion, he should ask himself if he showed responsibility by first gathering the needed facts, and then if he used those facts in a positive manner. A master realizes that the actions of a person are what is imperative in discovering his true intent.

Our government was established to fulfill a purpose. The running of the country is not in the hands of one person. The governmental body has three distinct parts: The Executive (President), the Legislative (the Senate and the House of Representatives), and the Judicial (the highest court in the land). This created the balance. Each part is a section of our government. Although each has a different function, they are one in purpose.

An example is when the economy of the country goes sour. The first judgment is on the President. Actually, the President's actions are mirroring our feelings and those of the representatives who we have elected in our governing bodies.

If we are not looking at the scope, we elect a different person in the office. In the next election, by putting another person in the position, the cycle goes on and on and on. We have to enhance what we already have to the next level of understanding. When we put the plight of the country on an elected official and then choose another, we are increasing the problem. Operating a country is not served best by a crash course. Four years in office, the person is just beginning to know the true implications of the job.

Every American is concerned with high taxes. Yet we seem to believe that raising taxes is the only way to support the country. What we don't realize is that in letting a president serve for only one term, we are increasing our debt. When a president relinquishes the position, we give him retirement, a staff, and security. We then take in a new president and offer him the salary worthy of the position and all the trappings that are associated with it.

We could be more informed concerning these issues, use our intuitive and creative source, and inform our leaders of what we think are the best methods to employ. This is done by realizing the empowerment which is in every one of us.

Another point is that we should never criticize another individual unless we have been in his predicament. We should embrace these individuals who have devoted many years in public office and respect their desire to lead their country into higher levels in the democratic way of life.

When we look at another person's manifestation, we have to always look for the intent of his decision and his actions. All of the masters share the same purpose: "To make the world a better place for you and me". It doesn't matter what position or talent they are involved in. It is the manner in which they use and manifest their talent.

When we are expressing our opinion, we must keep it in the context of the masters. We have to appreciate their calling of their hearts and use of their creative forces. We have to extend our empathy. We have to remember that in terms of the world's population, these representatives are few, and have an awesome responsibility to themselves and the rest of the world. We have to understand and fully comprehend the power of unity and oneness.

The masters give us a gift of their knowledge and love. As the receivers of such a gift, we have to turn our thoughts inward to the core of our being, and decide how we are going to cherish and use the gift. Since we are not sitting in the Oval Office, or in the music studio, we, like the masters, have to display a sense of trust in the universe and one another.

It is necessary to look at the magnitude of their offerings to the planet. Masters are not just extending their talent, and the results of their labor, simply with one country, but with the world. The interaction of this sharing is concerning themselves with many diverse people and elements of the planet.

During the history of our country, we have had many presidents of opposite parties and beliefs. However, their intent and purpose has always been the same. While we may have our own personal beliefs on how things should be done, we must never lose awareness of the fact that these brave and dedicated men are doing their best to ensure a life of freedom for our country and to extend that belief beyond the arbitrary boundary lines of our borders to the other continents of the globe. In following this pathway, our response should not be one of criticism, but of love, cooperation, and assistance. In doing this, our viewpoints are not judgmental and therefore are not of division but of unity.

Do you want to excel? If so, take the formula from the masters and apply it to any area in your life in which you desire success.

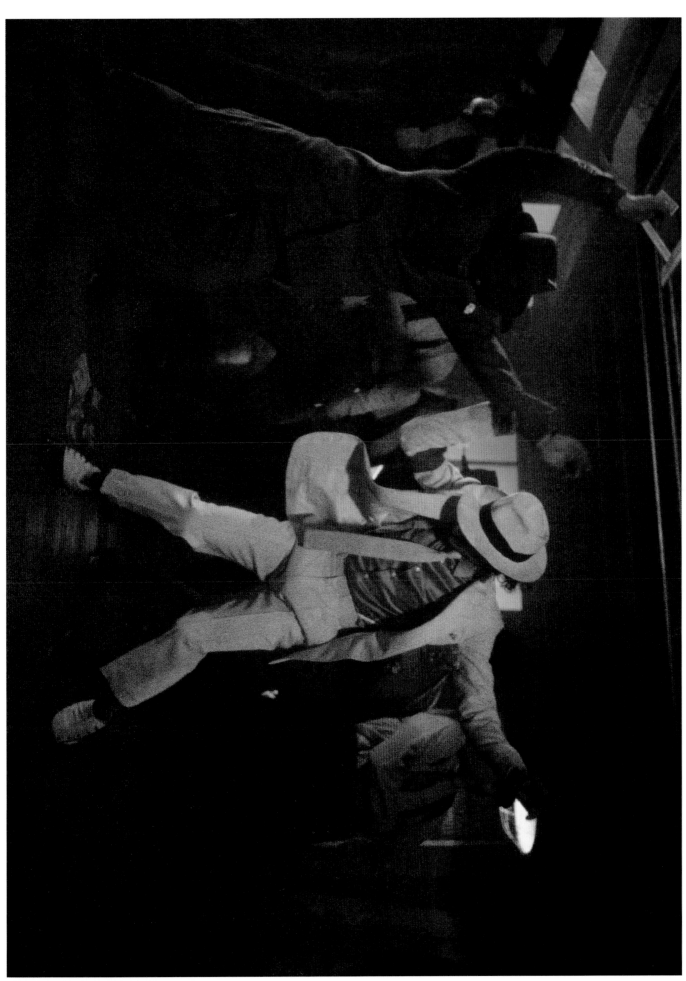

Photo Courtesy of MJJ Productions

Photo Courtesy of MJJ Productions

Chapter 9:

The Master's Solution to World Problems

"Revenge is alien to me."
Michael Jackson

$\mathcal{M}$ost people's solution to an injustice is receiving money. Money is nothing more than a symbol of work done, and to receive the services of another. If you buy a product, you are paying for all workmanship of the people involved and paying for the service of their performance. Money can never buy happiness. We think that what money buys may bring us excitement or pleasure. When we purchase something, it is the manifestation of the talent, effort, and work we applied to receive it. People who perfect their talent and advance their knowledge receive more benefit from their labors than those who do less.

People believe that if they have an injustice or wrong doing done to them, if they receive a monetary reward, it somehow equals the score. It never does. The author's experience appeared to have everything to do with money and nothing with what she did. The employer thought by letting her go, he would be able to maintain more of a profit.

He also thought by falsifying his records, he would receive a higher salary. He committed bigamy to have the opportunity to use someone else's money. In all of these instances, he did not work to the level of the money he was receiving. By doing the things that he did, everything backfired.

We constantly hear about people receiving large sums of money from a person that they feel harmed them in some manner. We must always ask the question, "Is your true and honest desire to make the wrong right, or see it as a easy way to attempt to receive something that had nothing to do with the infraction? Are you settling the score by receiving material gains that had to do with the victim's misfortune and believe that the physical enumeration is going to cure the emotional turmoil? It might simply serve to be a constant reminder of the pain and suffering.

The two personal experiences that were mentioned illustrate two concepts from the master that were expressed by Michael Jackson on his television interview. They are: (1) If you hear a lie over and over, you begin to believe it; and (2) Don't judge a person until you have talked with that person one on one.

Lately, society is attempting to solve many issues that were hiding inconspicuously in our homes and different places in society, the workplace and the government. In identifying them, we are moving ahead. In dealing with them if we are going to believe that we have the remedy by using the "catch as you catch can" philosophy, we are doing more harm than good, as all of us can become victims of making false judgments.

It is important to remember that masters have a thought process based on truth, and, therefore, are free from making false decisions or judgments. If we as a society think that we are solving the country's ills by criticizing another individual, we are making a horrendous mistake.

Where the master has been using his energy in directing his talent, he now has to divert that energy in restoring and maintaining his life's force. In not giving him our unbiased support, he begins to doubt the love and support that we so unselfishly bestowed upon him in the past. Remember, one thought can change the world. One detrimental thought misplaced can do the same thing with disastrous results in manifesting hurt and despair for the individual to whom it is directed.

When false judgments are made about another human being, we are doing worse than committing a murder because we have given that person the death sentence without knowing what really transpired. We are killing that person's spirit and attacking his soul. We always feel that a person who commits a physical crime be put to justice, but a person who kills another person's spirit and drive doesn't have to serve any sentence, make any restitution, or receive any training, so that the same actions are not repetitive.

It is time for a change in our method of thinking. When it comes for a judgment call on another one of our sisters or brothers, we might want to practice, "The best opinion is no opinion."

Righteousness always will prevail. Both the giver and receiver know this. The receiver will thrive in the long run, but has to feel the brunt of the giver's selfish actions. If he acted solely on his own, there wouldn't be a problem. The accuser always tries to enlist the support of others. The receiver, who is the innocent victim, while he has abundant sources of support, has to give his energy in neutralizing the environment that surrounds him.

Where is this energy originating? It is originating from the invisible thought system of people who think that power comes from expressing viewpoints that have no value, premise, or foundation. Masters receive their power from their knowledge and understanding of the universal laws that embrace them. We are our own best tool in finding the answers to the plights that are confronting our generation. We only have to look within ourselves.

We have to exhibit and extend empathy to our fellow man. One of the best ways to do this is to ask ourselves how we would like to be treated if we found ourselves in the same situation. In Michael's own words, he made the comment that he doesn't know anything for sure.

Michael was being extremely humble with this reply to Oprah Winfrey's question. This master knows music. He likes art. He spends time reading about the past and present masters. He gives physical form to his creativity. He can write. He can sing. He can dance. He knows a lot about the different cultures through his travel and tutor. He adores animals. He has developed an immense business empire. He loves children and all the people of the world.

Why was his response so appropriate? What did he mean?

He could mean that there is a lot in the world to learn. He could mean people and their ideas are always changing. He could be thinking about inventions and the sciences. We really don't know the reason for his reply. One area that the comment could apply is being unable to totally figure out people's thoughts and actions. Here, everyone has the power of choice and free will. We can't always know what those choices will be. When it comes to human nature, all of us know nothing for sure. This is the way it should be, as people don't always have to give the reasons for their actions and behavior, or fit into some norm. It's perfectly okay to be themselves. In fact, it's the highest quality of a true master!

When we judge a master, we are hurting our own expansion. A master always gives his gift in the form of his talent and the results of his labor. He always gives us his very best. When we falsely judge a master, we are cutting off his ability to share his best endeavors with us.

In the terms of the master, the best remedy to the world's issues is to handle them with love. Remember that love consists of acceptance and appreciation. There is always faith. Faith in the universe. Faith in the planet. Faith in our country, our brothers and sisters, but most of all, faith in ourselves. Whatever the situation, we can meet the challenge. A commitment to care and cherish one another by displaying our love is easy if we develop the qualities of the masters.

Well, we have been in similar situations. If we were to learn of someone who found himself in such a situation, we should reach out to that person with all the love and understanding that we could find within us.

We should attempt to go to that person and tell him to relax and let us feel his pain. When I was going through the experience, I didn't find anyone that had the same encounter. The doctors or even a therapist couldn't assist me, as I felt that they did not have the same experience and therefore, in all honesty, didn't know what I was feeling.

Sure, I could tell someone, and I did see a doctor and therapist. I received a bandaid in the form of Valium. It didn't remove the cause. Talking about the situation only solidified it, driving the details further into my mind. When I became stronger, the only thing I could do was release it and go on with my life.

I am fine now, but when something happens of a similar nature, the thoughts return; they always will, as the brain has immediate recall. When this happens, I smile and tell myself everything is okay and I get a sense of pride in my life. I made it through the difficult times, and like the children to whom I have dedicated my life's effort, I have survived.

Now I understand that a good therapist never tells one what to do; he asks questions which sharpen the thinking process in a specific area. The advantage of a therapist is that he is far removed from your personal life, and therefore can target one's thinking from any personal experiences both may have had. Family and friends may not always be able to do this due to their close, and loving, association.

In understanding others, we first have to respect and validate their feelings. Then, and only then, can we teach them the creative thinking process of the masters to enhance their own lives and the lives of others. The answers to the issues of our generation are not in criticizing our neighbor, but in perfecting ourselves so that we can reach out to others, take off the bandaid, and heal the wound!

I have a vision of establishing "Masters Workshops", so that the children of the world will have a better place in which to travel their life journey by knowing first-hand, the teachings of the masters.

My vision is vast. It would be having some of the masters come to be guest speakers and fill the auditoriums to the rafters. The sound would be deafening. The children would be screaming, "Here he comes, the King, the Master. Let us see you. What are you going to tell us? What are you going to do?"

Photo Courtesy of MJJ Productions

Like the master who uses day dreaming in the creation of ideas, the author's vision is unlimited. Just like there are various workshops or county fairs, she envisions master workshops where people can come and view the creative work of the masters. There would be meetings on the different arts with speakers to explain how they developed their craft. There would be people from the government who would tell the audience how they used the creative process in solving the many conflicts and issues facing our country.

The concepts that the master revealed would become apparent in all facets of our lives. It would be visible in all our encounters; from the government to the schools, to the colleges and universities, to the laboratories and to the workplace, and most significantly, in our homes. It's only a dream, but then, the master informs us that our dreams can come true. You know in your heart that he is right!

The master would close with, "Look. Look around you. Look at what you have done. Oh, it's so beautiful. Very powerful."

The children would fill churches. They would fill the school auditoriums. The crowds would fill the parks on a Sunday afternoon. Parents and teachers would flock to hear the messages. The masters have come to educate, share, depart knowledge, and unleash our creativity.

Would this change the world? Solve the issues? Create a better understanding among ourselves and other nations. Would it diminish the violence and bring harmony to a troubled world? Yes! Yes! Of course!
Where are the masters? Are they a lost breed? No, they are among us and doing quite well, thank you!

The universe helps us in many ways through the invisible realm. We have to understand that everything we see and hear isn't real. It has only been manifested in the real world by our creative source. Science tells us that matter is composed of atoms. These atoms break down into their counterparts and are dancing around in an energy field at such a rapid rate that everything appears to be solid. In these spaces the invisible source thrives.

When the universe is teaching, it uses the best and quickest method of exposure. This is the reason that we are hearing so much about the celebrities. The entertainment industry has been mentioned, but the government is having its fair share, due to their access to the media. We have to understand that what is happening to them is happening to people all over the world.

We are progressing. We are more knowledgeable of areas of concern. We must see the true purpose of the issue, and know that what we are seeing and hearing isn't real. What is real is that some people think they can get personal gain by twisting the true intention of the issue for their monetary benefit. This is where we, as a society, have to be knowledgeable and watch and protect the purity of our desire to make the world we live in, a better place. The examples are right before our eyes.

The true answers, however, are found in what we are not seeing and hearing. The media uses the creative source extremely well. First, it takes an event and adds color and interest by using adjectives and opinion. It believes that it is on to a very good thing. Next, we are seeing the media take it to a higher level in the tabloids.

The media is creating stories that at times have no foundation or merit. The sad part is that they are very convincing and we are not only buying the publication, but we are buying into information that in a lot of instances, doesn't exist.

It is not the intention of this message to criticize the media, but to educate the populace to always search for truth. This can be done by being mindful of the ability to distinguish fact from opinion, which is reflected in the degrees of sensationalism and the use of descriptive language. It is not necessary to change the media. What is crucial is discovering truth; what is factual from what is fiction. It is important to avoid the personal interpretation on the part of the commentator, unless, of course, we are engaging in a program that uses it as the format.

We always say we need the facts. What are we going to do with the limited amount of them that we are receiving? We can't do too much because we don't have the whole story. What we can do is to get more knowledge, not on the specific information, but in understanding the method used behind the scene.

Chapter 10:

The Making of a Master

"I don't know anything for sure. I'm still learning."
Michael Jackson

The book on this accomplished person, whom we know as Michael Jackson, has been completed. The conclusion is the discovery that all of us have the ability to become a master in our own life. We have the gift. All we need to do is to take off the wrapping that society has covered us up in, and use our inherent abilities, our creative process.

When the pretty ribbon and the colored paper are set aside, we are able to access the beauty of the object for what it really represents. We are able to discover its traits and the minute details which make it so valuable and contribute to its purpose.

The universe is always ready and willing to shower us with examples of our own creativity. Most of us believe that the result of our intuitive process must manifest in something big and dynamic. This isn't true. Ideas start with a small desire to create, change, or enhance a pre-existing thought, circumstance, condition, or situation.

Michael Jackson is one of the greatest manifestors of our time. He sees the scope of life in its entirety. He applies all the components of the intricate parts and combines them in ways to make the physical world work in harmony with his talent, service, and belief system.

The outstanding component of this man's success is in the manner he speaks when he expresses his viewpoint on a subject, whether it be in relationship to his talent or his opinion on an issue.

In the composition of the contents of the book much of the material was devoted to the style in which Michael speaks before his audience. The fashion in which he does this is consistent whether it be on his talent, cause, or adversity. It was interesting and educational to note that in all the times he has spoken publicly, he has never said an unkind or demeaning remark about another individual. He will speak of the plight of a condition, but not of another person. In this day and age, it is amazing. When adversity passes by, he never counter attacks -- ever.

Why does he respond in such a way? We would have to ask him. However, one reason might be that he looks for the best possible response that will help, not hinder, the circumstance. When we try to correct another individual, we are working on the wrong end of the spectrum. We intensify the problem. The cause has to be analyzed; otherwise we are using the bandaid mentality.

We can always recognize who we are in our evaluation of others. If we see our own goodness and potential in ourselves, we can see it in the people with whom we associate. When we feel insecure and react with such feelings toward others, and when we use the outward display of force to make others see our opinion, the unyielding attitude is using the false sense of ourselves. We are drawing on the outside influence of others instead of the peaceful intuitive source that resides within us.

When a person has to argue, he keeps the cycle going in order to defend himself. The real issue somehow gets lost. If what you believe is important enough to voice a request or give an opinion, your conviction will be acknowledged by the other person in the soft, but intense manner in all phrases of the communication, including your body language.

All we have to do in speaking with others is to express how we feel so that the individual with whom we are interacting can absorb our intentions. When we get excited and have to draw on constituents other than ourselves, we lose the listener's ability to grasp the message. In attempting to try and defend ourselves, the other person not only has to ascertain your behavior, but begin the task of defending his own position. At this time, nothing positive transpires. There becomes a total breakdown, not only in communication, but in finding a solution to the topic as both parties become involved in defending themselves.

Another misconception is that we believe to remain silent or walk away from an unpleasant situation is a sign of weakness. Nothing is further from the truth. It shows the greatest power of all which is restraint. Anyone can open his mouth or use his fists. This isn't showing control but exercising a lack of such within oneself. When a person exercises silence with another, it is creating the space for each party to take more time to evaluate the topic.

A valuable asset of exercising restraint is letting the other person know that in your own viewpoint and life, it isn't really that important. If your family, friend, or business associates feel differently, that's all right with you. In no sense is it giving in to the other person if you don't agree. It doesn't mean that the interaction won't be discussed or an action taken at a later time.

In fact, it may have a greater impact. It may keep the other person attempting to guess or figure out what your future actions will be. This being the case, he may think enough about the encounter to find a suitable solution and approach you on the results of his understanding.

A master realizes that he is independently dependent. What in the world does this mean, to be independently dependent? It means that we may be independent in managing the direction of our lives, but we are dependent upon others for their services.

As we grow and expand physically and emotionally, as our understanding of the universe increases, we become able to make more and more choices about ourselves and the society in which we live. It also infers that we take more and more responsibility for those choices.

Psychologists are telling us that we are the ones who are responsible for our accomplishments and how we expand and grow. We are responsible for the development of our talents and the positions we hold. This is very true.

In the contemporary era in which we are living, we have become more and more dependent upon the services of others for our survival and well being. A master is very much aware of the necessity of relying on the services of others to meet his needs. These services might include the area of his individual talent. However, he knows that the masters of the world perform in the capacity to meet his personal needs.

Michael couldn't operate without these people who are talented in their own endeavors. He uses many of the services from the genius of their labor and commitment to their craft. One just has to follow the master through his daily activities to see how much he relies on them. All this is apparent in his lifestyle. Who maintains the display of his manifestations? Probably the number is in the hundreds. How is he able to travel in his lear jet? Someone had to design it. The pilot has to be highly efficient in serving in his capacity, and stay current on his knowledge of modern aviation.

Who landscapes those beautiful gardens? Who takes care of the animals? Who designs and sews his outfits? Who created and maintains the utility plants that bring in those necessities? Who shops and prepares his food? Who designed and brought the furniture and art into his home? Do you get the idea? Of course, the list would be more or less endless.

The problem is that people who work in service or support positions don't see the magnitude of their own contributions and attainments. Doing anything well, and to classify as master quality, takes the following: (1) Education and training; (2) Use of the intuitive force; (3) Teamwork; (4) Dedication; and (5) Commitment.

Everyone knows the value of an education and proper training. We believe it so much that we encourage everyone to get a higher degree in learning. This sounds good, but is it practical in every situation? Its value depends on the individual's makeup and the job one is seeking. It is by no means the only way.

Here again, the giver and receiver concept can apply. When you attend college, the professor gives you the results of his studying and training. As the receiver of the knowledge, its value will be dependent on its usage on a personal level. How is the person who receives the gift going to apply it? Is getting the education the sole accomplishment? Is it isolated and not integrated into the totality of the individual? Is it used as being an authority on a particular subject but has no practical application?

The other way of getting educated is by being both the giver and receiver to yourself. You tune into your natural talent and seek the means which will enable its practical application. It may be a specialized school. It may be going to the library and studying up on the subject. It may be getting a starting job in your field of interest and being the very best that you can, thereby working your way up the corporate ladder. It may be learning from the masters who serve as your mentors.

The means that one employs is not the deciding factor. What is important is that the education and training are integrated to be fulfilling to you and an enhancement to the planet. Strangely, the masters usually do it in this manner. These people have an extraordinary desire to achieve by using and cultivating their natural talent. Michael Jackson revealed how the masters work. They claim their space and get the most out of it. No matter what your talent or service is, work and know more about it than any other person alive.

True education is an ongoing process, and is necessary in all areas of our lives and throughout our life span on the planet. It keeps us vitalized and our brain active. There is always a new, different, and more advanced way of doing things. Usually, the results reflect a quicker and a more efficient way.

To illustrate this point once again, the history of transportation can be studied. It used to take the pioneers months to travel from coast to coast, if they were fortunate enough to combat disease, hunger, the weather, and other adversities. Today, you can get to any location on the globe in a matter of hours.

Photo Courtesy of MJJ Productions

Any advancement for the betterment of mankind is noble. Any invention that kills or cripples innocent people is not worthy, no matter how we attempt to justify its usage. The more advanced our creative resources become, the more judicious we must be. We must protect ourselves and reserve the right for people of all nations to do likewise.

The true solutions come in the form of education, example, communication, and negotiation. Here, like with everything else, we have to determine the internal cause. If it is poor leadership, we target our actions toward the leaders and not the innocent citizens that reside in the country.

People who show dedication and commitment to a belief in themselves will succeed. Both the dedication to a creative idea and the commitment to see it through to its completion will reflect in the ability to overcome the hurdles. Dedication can be thought of as agreement with yourself and your purpose in life. Commitment to the purpose serves as an illustration to others of your intention to finish whatever you have started or enhance any gift that is given to you.

In order to get your talent out into the far corners of the planet, you are going to have to team up with some person, or group of persons, who can take your talent or project to the next stage of development. You do the basics and pass it on to the next master for completion. In this stage, the ideas remain yours. You are still the overseer. You still contribute to the whole but you need the expertise of others with whom you trust to enhance the resulting project of your original manifestation. A master is skillful in the recruitment of others.

Photo Courtesy of MJJ Productions

By this time, you are beginning to believe that you have the potential of becoming a master over your own life. It feels good and rewarding because you know that you are a valuable component of the world. You have read about the traits and thought process of an accomplished master. To determine your talent, develop it, and share it with others aren't the only criteria in having mastery over your life. There are more qualifications. Let's go back and look at them and evaluate them by putting them in question form to ourselves:

1. Do I have control over my own life by focusing on what is important? By focusing on my own actions, do I help to affect others in a positive manner?

2. Have I developed my talent to the best of my ability? What others may think of my talent is not the deciding factor. Am I satisfied with my accomplishment?

3. Have I expanded on the original talent or idea? Was I able to exceed the normal and arbitrary boundaries that were limiting my own creativity?

4. Have I discovered my purpose and my talent? Am I using my purpose and talent for the betterment of those with whom I associate, and mankind in general?

5. Do I live my life by being an example to others which is in harmony with my own belief system?

6. Am I putting back into the environment in ratio to the portion that I am using?

7. Do I realize that I am a result of nature or a Higher Source than man?

8. Do I have a clear understanding of the laws of the universe? Do I look for examples that are manifested by nature? Do I feel a close relationship to nature's energy force? Do I fully comprehend the wonderness of the creation of children that I bring into the world? Do I not only see them as an extension of my mate and myself, but as a gift to us, and our contribution to the planet? Do I realize that my task is to mold and refine this gift, helping them to discover and use their own creativity?

9. Do I work to enhance the world by developing the space that I occupy to the best of my ability? Are other people glad to be in my presence?

10. Am I taking full advantage of the invisible power of intuition, inspiration, and thought? Am I aware and acting on these invisible forms of my creativity?

11. Am I putting into the physical realm the results of my education and training?

12. Am I able to ascertain the truth from the opinions of other sources so that I am not reacting by making false decisions or judgments?

If you have mastered the twelve qualifications, there is still one ingredient that must be added to the steps, and that is to perform all of the factors in an act of love.

To exhibit master qualities, all of our endeavors have to be done with purity of purpose, focused and fulfilled with the desire to do them with an act of love both for ourselves and each encounter we surmount. With this as our goal, it will permeate throughout the task at hand and the individuals we associate with in fulfilling our obligations, desires, and ambitions.

Photo Courtesy of MJJ Productions

Chapter 11:
Epilogue

"You can't do your best when you are doubting yourself."
Michael Jackson

The journey is complete, and what a wonderful journey it was! The greatest aspect in any endeavor is the participation a person gives to a cause to which he is firmly committed. The giving of the self, in offering assistance to others, always reaps and manifests its own reward.

In the past few years, the author has been keenly aware of the negative information we are receiving into our homes. The belief is that by reporting and identifying problems, the solution will automatically rectify itself. We are rarely getting at the cause. The thought came to the author that instead of simply being aware, she had to act upon her concerns. She somehow had to change the tide.

In the first chapter of Michael's book, *Moonwalk*, he mentioned the power of telling stories, and the fact that it can take the listener anywhere emotionally, with something as deceptively simple as words. The English vocabulary is full of words that have been used for centuries. What makes words so unique is that they can be combined in millions of arrangements to create new ideas and meaning.

Communication has always been fascinating. The sharing of ideas is one of two ways of learning. We learn by the knowledge of the masters, by hearing and reading and doing research on their accomplishments. We are also able to learn by the manifestations of their creativity.

When the idea became apparent to write about the masters, a commitment was made to not follow the usual literary style of modern times when writing about individuals. The author knew before she began that she would never mention anything negative or harmful, because it would not only defeat her purpose, but would not be in harmony with her own belief system. While she would never write anything detrimental or cause the subject additional suffering and pain, she could very easily, in following the teachings of the masters, use herself as an example.

If you want to learn and really understand about the master, Michael Jackson, the answers have been discussed. You see, there is a parallel in all of our lives. Some of the answers are between the spaces of the lines, but they are there. It was purposely done this way to let you draw your own conclusions and find that space within you that allows peace, faith and contentment. We have to open up our hearts and become an empty vessel, so the good concepts can enter and consume us with love and understanding and let it flow outward as our gift to the planet. If we don't do this, we are dying a little bit inside every time we sit in judgment of another individual. We have compromised ourselves by not using our own intuitive and natural talents, and we have attempted to explain to others how worldly and wise we are, by putting a brother or sister down. The scale is uneven. It is unbalanced. It is tipped and becomes unable to ground itself.

The true solution to the ills of the world is to open ourselves up, stretch out our arms and reach toward the sky, and make a wish to make a better world. We are the world. We are the rich and famous. We are the poor and the impoverished. We are the talented and the creative. We are the sick and the healthy. Within our bodies, we are a little bit of everything, and we are the remedy to our world.

We can't slide downward. We have to increase our abilities and keep an eye on that invisible spot in the sky like the tree. There is no beginning or ending. We have to go the full circle of our experience. We start by showing compassion and understanding toward our fellow man.

Discovering the traits of the master gave the author a greater reward than anything monetary could ever do. It gave her insight to the qualifications of this master through studying his manifestations, talent, creativity, sensitivity, and his close association with the elements of the universe.

As a society, we have to stop the issues from multiplying. We have to become one in our thoughts, words, and deeds. We have to comprehend the principle that there is a constant balance operating in the universe. We hear constantly that we have to get our act together, so future generations can enjoy the same benefits that we are receiving. However, we have to still be able to enjoy the planet while we are here. Our time is not over yet!

The balance is understanding that the adults share their wisdom of their age, and balance it with the boundless energy of the young. We are their guides. We point out, we show, we illustrate, and most importantly, we help them to use their own uniqueness and creativity. We are generous with our praise, and soft and tender in pointing out any inconsistencies or flaws. Above all, we delight in our interactions with one another!

In handling and coping with unpleasant circumstances, we have to change our thinking process and think of them as lessons that the universe has determined that we are ready to learn. We have to reach out and admit that we don't know all the answers; that the thought process we are producing in the physical world does not depict a complete understanding; that life is still a mystery and challenges us to keep on exploring its wonders.

Many nights the author would sit up in the confines of her little office and listen to Michael's albums. She would often wonder what in the world she was doing. Where the thoughts were coming from; it was as if she were reaching way down into another part of herself and let her own creativity free from the normal daily patterns that enslave us.

As mentioned before, the author has learned the value of seeing a competent therapist. You know, when the master wants an unbiased opinion, he seeks out the advice of others. It is the same with the people who hold high-level positions in the government; they have their own advisors. A good therapist should be held in high esteem. This person helps one sort out one's feelings and emotions, thus enhancing the decisions one makes in life.

During our time on the planet, every person should have someone that he has confidence in to help explore his thinking process, other than someone with whom that person is deeply involved. This could be a minister or someone in a chosen field whose opinion he trusts and values. Doing this should never be seen as a form of weakness, but rather strength and a desire to enhance one's life in an earnest effort to make the correct decisions by examining his thinking process in a specific area. This is in harmony with the master's statement, that he doesn't know everything. One should never be afraid to seek out information from others who are on a different plateau than oneself. This is a highly beneficial way to increase personal knowledge.

Michael has spent much time with Diana Ross. When the author was thinking of how she would heal the world, she remembered a time that she saw Miss Ross perform in Lake Tahoe. A large part of the performance centered around a song that held a very good bit of advice. The lyrics told us to "Reach out and touch someone's hand; Make this world a better place, if you can." All of us should extend a helping hand to each other. Then, and only then, can we experience the oneness we share and the common bond that binds us together.

Photo Courtesy of MJJ Productions

Photo Courtesy of MJJ Productions

Chapter 12:

A Note from the Author

"What one wishes is to be touched by truth."
Michael Jackson

This book is the first of its kind. It is unique because in the first section of the book, it discussed the teachings of a master. Michael Jackson, and his phenomenal contributions to the planet, including, but not limited to his talent, creative process, his humanitarian efforts, his astute awareness to the issues facing our century, and most of all, his solution to their demise which reflects in love.

The second section of the book used the author as an example, but yet was, in truth, speaking of the master and anyone whose experience parallels hers. Any experience we encounter is given to us for a purpose. It develops our understanding of the experience, but more importantly, it gives us a greater sensitivity, and knowing that within our being, we hold the resources to conquer the vicissitudes of life.

The planet is suffering from the ills of its inhabitants. All the issues haven't been addressed in this book. The true solution, however, is the same. Until we can operate from the core of our inner self and find a place that is not judgmental can we truly be our best and serve others.

Many people have asked the author why she chose Michael Jackson as her subject. The primary reason is that he is such a good study for the manner in which he is manifesting his life. Throughout the book, the author has made the association between the giver and the receiver. It is her belief that many of us are not handling the gift of the master in proper perspective. We are quick to form an opinion without studying the manner that celebrities respond to the various conditions that they are experiencing.

When Michael was asked why he exhibited certain motions in his dancing, he said that he becomes a part of the music. When the author wanted to understand why Michael responds to situations in the manner in which he does, she researched his responses. In concerning herself with his actions and viewpoints, she learned a great deal about the person. All of his outward actions and responses are in perfect harmony to his beliefs. The outstanding feature is that they are consistent and are not affected by the problem or task at hand.

Many people use adjectives of "weird, bizarre, and elusive". These descriptive words do not reveal his true essence. When Michael Jackson believes he has an offering for the planet, he is open and generous. In attempting to discover the desire to elevate Michael Jackson to the select group of masters, the author realized that in order to truly heal the world and continue her passion of her craft, children need the example of a master.

In her selection of using an example, one had to be chosen with whom the general public was familiar, especially the youth. The public's reaction could immediately be the response, "Michael Jackson?". The answer was the same as that of the master, "And why not?".

Most people form their opinions from their knowledge. It is crucial for them to contemplate where the source of their opinions originate. More than not, they originate from the opinions of others exhibiting their craft in a very small and limited manner.

In order to undertake a project as big as establishing an American Master, the characteristics of a master had to be determined. This was done by creating a list of the qualifications or the attributes of a master. Next, it required reading about the past masters and reading all the material on the present subject. This took a huge amount of effort and time.

It was interesting because the information of the past masters was based on fact and not the opinions of the specific author(s). When I turned to read about Michael Jackson, other than his accomplishments reflecting his talent, the information was based on the opinion of the writer of the information. Further, when references were listed in books, they were based on the interpretation of those interviewed by the authors.

Michael's advice is to not judge a person unless you have talked to that person one on one. Keeping that statement in mind as the material was assimilated, all the materials concerning Michael came from him, either in the form of his book *Moonwalk*, his short films, and his television interviews with Oprah Winfrey and Diane Sawyer. Statements in the book were expanded, and void of opinion of this author.

In studying a person of the stature of Michael Jackson, it is important to be aware that, although he has developed his talent to the highest degree, he is still a human being. He has the same emotions, trials, and criticisms that all of us share, and many of them are the same faced by previous masters. They, too, could have been thought of as being weird, elusive, or bizarre because their thought processes and manifestations were on a higher plane than the average population. Let us not make the same mistake. Let's keep the talent and work of Michael Jackson in the proper perspective and learn all we can from this astute and generous person. Then, we have taken our own thought process to the next level of expansion.

All of our life experiences are presented to us to increase our understanding of the universe. They make us look for solutions, make choices, and nurture ourselves. Michael, after a long absence from public view, once again opened up his heart and life to us, and in doing so, made himself extremely vulnerable. This takes true courage. He is, once again, sharing his life's experiences with the public. What an opportunity for the populace to admire and learn!

He has given us a priceless gift. It is of such magnitude that most of us don't know how to accept it. In our earnest desire, we want more information, so we latch on to any news of the master and lose our true focus.

Recently, there have been new experiences in Michael's life. The true information that we should be searching for is not the circumstances, but how he copes with and solves them. Michael knows how to deal with them in a very effective way. He stays loyal to the inner core of his being and true essence.

Always remember, our true advancement is not in what we know, but what the lessons are and how to apply them in our lives. Michael draws on the core of his being and heart and finds the best choice by not losing sight of his true character and essence. There is no better current example than what can be learned by studying the recent experiences that Michael has endured. Michael always uses sensitivity and softness in his demeanor, and in his presence before the public. This is so amazing. The world may attack, but Michael looks for serenity and care in his interaction of creating the peace he desires in his public and private life. A master's actions are always consistent with his core beliefs.

After reading the message of the book, it's time for you to focus on its purpose. Is the book really about Michael Jackson as we look, listen, and attempt to further our understanding of his life?

It depends on how much you desire to know. In choosing the subject, it was necessary to transcend the physical personage of the man. It had to search far beyond this realm to get his true essence.

In working with children, when they become upset with me and comment, "I don't like you," they are asked why. They respond with such answers as, "I don't like the way you look. I don't like what you want me to do. I don't like what you are saying."

They are asked the question, "Are you really seeing me, and know what you are seeing, and hearing what is really me? What you think you are seeing and hearing isn't me; it's my envelope. If you want to really understand what I'm all about, open up the envelope and read the letter!"

Photo Courtesy of MJJ Productions

This is the way the masses look at the master. They are always concerned about his physical appearance and actions. This isn't where the answers lie in furthering our knowledge. The true essence is inside the envelope, and is found in his message depicted through his talent. In order to comprehend the individual, it is important to look beyond what we are seeing and hearing and basing our opinion on them.

In having an opinion based upon a solid and accurate foundation, we have to look at the invisible forces and research the thought process. The answers aren't found in the manifestations, but rather through the thought process. It commences with the manner in which Michael Jackson uses the intuitive and creative sources, and his ability to be inspired by the provisions of the universal force that resides within his being and results in his contributions to the physical world.

Possibly, if we were to have an audience before him and asked him how he has reached the height of attainment that he has, he would tell us that he has already given us his answers.

Did he? Where do we capture them? You may be able to find them by going back and looking at the quotations and lyrics, and studying them. The true answers are between the lines. What does he mean when he says, "He doesn't know anything for sure." What does he mean to use wisdom, or that he thinks of himself as an instrument of nature?

Perhaps, Elizabeth Taylor knew her friend very well when she described him as being generous, giving, and caring. Maybe the answers will come when we realize what we are looking for, we will find. If we limit our study on what we are seeing, our search is one of limitation and not abundance.

We may discover that in forming opinions, we are mirroring our beliefs about ourselves and not Michael Jackson. We have to admit to ourselves that in some way, while we are curious, we are a little jealous that he has reached such attainment and we are rather stuck in our physical bodies, creativity, and lifestyle.

In a sense, the answer is in our use of measurement and dividing our time of life in stages. Here, the solution may be in realizing the profound message that Michael gives us to evaluate our interaction with children. When we see the world in the eyes of the children, whose wonderment and innocence of life are the foundation for their creativity, we realize we should keep such characteristics at the core of our being. In truth, we remain children until the time we have conquered all the mysteries of life. We may have to be willing to spend a lifetime searching for them.

In our relationship with the masters, it was mentioned that we have to do our part and give them our respect, appreciation, and acceptance in the form of our love. When there is a major change in the master's life, we remain loyal and continue to shower our devotion. It was previously mentioned in the first half of the book, that if you can understand the actions, you can understand the person. Michael comprehends the principles of a master. When a new event takes place in the master's life, we have to be careful in the use of projection. We, like Michael, have to realize we don't know everything.

A master does not operate on the belief of scarcity or limitation. Michael has said that he loves all people of all races all over the world. A master realizes what he wants from the planet, he has to put it out to multiply and return to him. If he wants to be respected for his talent and love, those are the elements he will continue to put into circulation. In fact, these new experiences will no doubt give him added emotion, sensitivity and feeling in his stage persona.

We have to be cognizant that every one of us experience the same ups and downs of life, regardless of the positions that we hold. One of the misconceptions of the population is that they stand in awe of people who have reached the epitome of success and feel that they should, due to their status, be perfect specimens in acting out the drama of their lives. In truth, that is exactly what they are. Reaching perfection is not the events in our lives, but how we respond to them. In this regard, Michael is a perfect role model.

The author has given her gift of the planet to the reader. What he chooses to do after receiving it is totally up to him. Like the gift of talent from the performer, he can learn from the experience, enjoy it, consider it of little value, or use it as one of the means to change his life.

Our life on the planet is a journey. The author hopes that the contents of the book took the reader on an exciting trip and pointed out some of the scenic points of interest along the way. She would like to mention that her love and devotion to Michael Jackson is not one of a fan, but rather of gratitude; one of a student listening and learning from the master. What a teacher he is! He not only lives according to his beliefs, but is willing to share them with his universal family. A master, through his medium, changes lives by his example.

A master's philosophy of life remains consistent because it's the foundation of his being. During his lifetime, he will take his basic philosophy and enhance it, but the constituents will never change. By being such a profound teacher, he has added to the author's understanding and sharpened her own thinking process in a manner that no monetary equivalent could equal. He taught that no formal education, no life experiences are of ultimate value unless we balance them with our intuitive self. He also taught the author to develop her talents and be willing and vulnerable to share them with the world in which she is an integral part. He illustrated that truth is balancing what we know with that we don't, and the true answers are somewhere inbetween.

A master always sets and displays the proper example of whatever he is attempting to achieve in life, and avoids condemnation The example is always compatible with this purpose and reflects in his value of life. Michael's talent is reflected in his music, but his purpose in life is presented in his communication through that medium and his manifestation on the planet.

The manner in which he is fulfilling his purpose is by attempting to heal the world of its wounds. The issues of a wounded world are many. Before we can do any healing on a permanent and consistent basis we must get at the cause. Michael desires to see a world of unity. This unity has to be examined in its entirety. If we realize our life is a gift, both for ourselves and to enhance the planet, we have to see the scope of things. Unity, in its purest form, brings everything into a sense of oneness.

In realizing the gift of life, you transmit that belief to all living things. In realizing that one principle, the world can be transformed into the beautiful place that Michael has envisioned. If we value our own life, we are going to be extremely careful with our association with all living things; people, animals, plants, the works!

The master has the thought process needed to change the world. He has enlightened us by the use of his talent and the means that he has ready and able to use at his disposal. The lyrics for *Man in the Mirror* tell us where we should begin. Michael's generous contributions in donating his time and effort, and his financial assistance to worthy causes show us the path we should travel.

In concerning our interactions with each other, he has told us to use caution in forming judgments. Healing the world is a gigantic task if we work on each issue as an unrelated segment to the other problem lurking around the corner. It would be like not attending to the source of a fire and containing it, and having to run around and put out all of the secondary fires.

If we follow the philosophy of the master, it's really simple. The solution is in treating each person with the same sensitivity and love that we hold for ourselves. If we were to work with a sense of unity and share what we know is true about ourselves, there would be no hunger, no wars, no violence, no AIDS, no drugs, and most important, no factions among us.

The solution sounds so easy. The problem is we try and make it difficult by thinking selfishly of our own desires. We do not fully comprehend that if we work in unity most of what we really need will be met; not in the realm of limitation but in abundance; both for our neighbors and ourselves.

Michael showed the author that she must give back to the planet in an equal ratio of what she is using. While he is giving millions of dollars to worthy causes, she should be willing to share her dollars to causes that are important. He has made her realize that a soft, gentle, natural demeanor is the best approach in interacting with others, and that silence may be the best course of action.

On the very last page of his autobiography, *Moonwalk*, Michael reveals the primary motives of a master. It has been years since the book was published and his philosophy remains the same:

"What one wishes is to be touched by truth and to be able to interpret that truth so that one may use what one is feeling and experiencing, be it despair or joy, in a way that will add meaning to one's life and will hopefully touch others as well. This is art in its highest form. Those moments of enlightenment are what I continue to live for."[45]

In attending his concerts, Michael's fans get the picture and honor his accomplishments. The banners, the chanting, the tee-shirts and jackets, all proclaim their love and understanding of his excellence. While they are seeing the outward manifestation of his creative source, they are getting a glimpse of his soul, which is expressed by his deep feeling and sensitivity. Yes, he is Michael, "The King of Pop". He is now Michael, "A Master of Our Generation."

Photo Courtesy of MJJ Productions

One Hundred Two Guidelines
from the
Master's Handbook

"He who arms himself with love
wins every fortune."[46]

- Michelangelo

One Hundred Two Guidelines

1. Share your desire and purpose in life with others.

2. Seek to have a deeper understanding of the universe.

3. Realize that your earning power is in direct relationship to your effort.

4. Know the value of a true friend.

5. Have goals and use intuition, inspiration, and thought.

6. Create new ideas and expand on them.

7. Balance the spiritual and physical world.

8. Take advantage of opportunity.

9. Be relaxed, honest, and sincere when communicating with others.

10. Teach others by your example.

11. Use your own experiences in making a point with others. Don't demean the other person.

12. Take pride in your total being, your environment, your country, and your heritage.

13. Take responsibility for your own actions.

14. Realize that all human beings are the same.

15. Know that all of us, in truth, are brothers and sisters.

16. Be aware that all human beings are one with the universe.

17. Understand the reciprocal relationship between the "giver" and the "receiver".

18. Believe in your innate ability to create.

19. Know the difference between what you already know and what is foreign to your own understanding.

20. Study the talent of the past and present masters.

21. Know the value of networking and association with people of equal ability or better.

22. Look for the positive side of situations and avoid the negative in thought, word and deed.

23. Believe that our country is one of the most advanced countries of the world, where it is easy to manifest your dreams.

24. Avoid taking into heart the unfavorable comments of others.

25. Search for the truth and be selective in your thoughts.

26. Understand that where we place our thoughts and energy becomes our reality.

27. View the consistency of nature and apply it to your actions.

28. Notice that the world is always ready for a new and innovative manner in manifesting.

29. Attain perfection within yourself so that your ability to solve issues can become refined.

30. Use creativity in all your endeavors in relationship with your talent.

31. Take time for recreation, for diversion and space to enhance your ability to create.

32. Spend time daydreaming, as it is a vital part of the creative source.

33. Have mentors who can help you and teach you the important elements of your own creativity.

34. Manifest creativity in your personal life and surroundings, as well as in your vocation.

35. Claim your rightful space in life, and work all the elements of the space to your advantage.

36. Know more about the subject of your talent than anyone else.

37. Develop and expand your talent in the fields of business and services.

38. Live a lifestyle that is comfortable and enjoyable in meeting your own needs and desires.

39. Be willing to give back to the planet, a portion of the blessings that you received, both in the form of profit and the dedication to a worthwhile cause.

40. Assist people who are less fortunate than yourself, whether it be emotional, financial, or health.

41. Remember to be a constant role model for others.

42. Realize that the home is a sacred place where you have the permission to be your true self.

43. Know that you are an instrument of nature and there is a Higher Source guiding you.

44. Know that using projection and judgment are misleading in attempting to exact understanding and motives of another person.

45. Study the children, as they are the greatest teachers because of their innocence and wonderment of life.

46. Setting the mood is the first step in good communication.

47. Keep an open mind. Remember, we know nothing for sure.

48.   Believe in wishes and your ability to make them come true.

49.   Trust yourself, for only then can you trust in others, and they in you.

50.   Learn how to use disappointment and pressure to an advantage.

51.   Always be selective in securing a reliable source to get information or share ideas.

52.   Understand the value of love and that it is based on respect, acceptance, and appreciation.

53.   Remain humble in the midst of the audience.

54.   Remember, at times, silence is more effective than speaking, and carries a message of its own.

55.   Converse only when you have some message to convey.

56.   Realize that putting down someone's character and life force is destroying a part of you, and you will lose an equal part of yourself.

57.   Be your natural self and reflect your own personality.

58.   Understand that money is a symbol of honest labor and will manifest in physical form or benefits of equal likeness.

59.   Know that the payment of money will never appease the receiver if it only enhances his physical environment and never satisfies the soul.

60.   Find the solutions to problems from within and transmit them to the environment.

61.   Realize that you can never make another individual change; that such change resides within the individual and a desire to do so.

62.   Judging another individual without conversing with him will not give an honest and accurate appraisal.

63. Use your own talent and creativity to enhance your own personal lifestyle and surroundings.

64. Learn and apply the techniques and passions from the previous masters.

65. Set goals for yourself and stretch them beyond their regular boundaries.

66. Allow people the option of sharing what they feel is necessary, pertinent, and interesting in their own lives, and allow them the right to live a life of privacy.

67. Give children the opportunity to be themselves and understand that education and guidance starts when they are very young.

68. See that children have the opportunity to be heard and respected.

69. Acknowledge and associate with people of your caliber who share in the goals that you are achieving.

70. Learn from the principles of the universe and apply those very same principles in your own life.

71. Take time to nurture yourself and the components of the planet.

72. In discussing a sensitive subject, use yourself or a neutral subject as an example.

73. Use empathy and understanding in correcting or guiding another individual; not force, manipulation, nor the ego.

74. Choose a marriage partner who is compatible with your goals in the physical and spiritual realm of your life.

75. Comprehend the true essence of life; that there are very few absolutes in the creative source.

76. Know that the ability to create uses the invisible components of intuition, inspiration and thought, can be applied in all aspects of your life.

77. Believe that the universe manifests whatever it receives. Caution has to be used with this concept because it will produce both the good and the bad, the right and the wrong.

78. Use your time on the planet wisely to develop, grow, and expand.

79. Listen to the words of the master when he tells you that each of us has the ability to make our dreams come true.

80. Applying revenge, or making someone "pay" for something they had done, is alien to the masters.

81. Advancing in our own endeavors takes hard work, sacrifice, and commitment.

82. To become complete and experience all the joys of the world, it is necessary to complete all the stages of development. If a stage is missed, it is advantageous to go back, learn, and enjoy the missing step.

83. Gather all the information and facts before giving an opinion.

84. Looking and evaluating another person's behavior without being asked is mirroring your own shortcomings and insecurities.

85. Judging a person's character, assets, and philosophy is not revealed by his physical appearance and can be very misleading.

86. Concentrate on the important aspects of life and let the small, incidental annoying things pass.

87. Focus on the task at hand by exercising concentration and purpose.

88. Have a keen sense of timing when interacting with another individual.

89. Work at an activity to its completion, and attain perfection in your own mind.

90. Take control of your own projects, and don't let outside influences attempt to change your inherent ability to create and reach your desired attainment.

91. Seek to understand the true motives of an individual's suggestions or actions.

92. Use "Behavior Modification" in assisting another individual to change his actions because then he is free to make his own choices.

93. Realize that in correcting an infraction, the best solution is in educating and training, and not in believing that retaliation is always the best deterrent.

94. Get your own empowerment through your own endeavors and not at the sacrifice of exercising control or power over another individual.

95. Understand that the family is the nucleus of early learning, viewpoints, and foundation for our creativity.

96. Use caution in stereotyping, labeling, and categorizing people into specific groups.

97. Know that we are perfectly adapted to enjoy all of the attributes, elements, and conditions to sustain us and are present for our success.

98. Know that the masters are present in our day and age.

99. In accepting an attribute, you are accepting the totality of the individual.

100. Operate from a place of love and extend that love out to others by accepting their uniqueness, strengths, and frailties.

101. Know that if the character of an individual doesn't change, that in truth, the reputation of an individual remains constant.

102. Realize that perfection is not determined by the events in your life, but in the choice of the solution.

Photo Courtesy of MJJ Productions

A portion of the proceeds of the sales of

Michael Jackson American Master

will be donated to the charity of the master's choice

Acknowledgments

The author would like to give her appreciation and thanks to the following people who have given their guidance, expertise, and love:

Mr. Michael Jackson, who displayed trust in someone unknown to him and was responsive to her desire to give her gift to the planet. The commitment to his craft, his understanding of universal principles, and his efforts to "Heal the World" made the teachings of the book possible.

Mr. Bob Jones of MJJ Productions, who graciously secured permission for me to write the book, and whose association I honor and revere. Michael has the good fortune to employ persons who exhibit the qualities of the master in their respective fields. Mr. Jones is such a person. He is quick, skilled, and knowledgeable in making decisions and wears a multitude of hats.

Ms. Kimberley Ingram of MJJ Productions, who so warmly and graciously received me. She is a fine example of and complement to the world of the masters.

Mr. Walt Love of R & R Communications, whose knowledge in his field is excelled by none. While Michael is the "King of Pop", Walt Love is the "King of Disc Jockeys". His long tenure in the industry revealed a wealth of information which was extremely helpful. He is a vital extension of an artist's talent, and to whom a large part of one's success is dependent upon.

Mr. & Mrs. Bernard Anderson, whose time, love, and devotion made the completion of the book possible. I first met them in one of the youth homes which I managed. Bernard taught me the value of good counseling, of life, its purpose, and the skill to direct my talents. Cathi illustrates, silently, the methods of standing behind the man in one's life. These two people I consider part of my family, and I delight in the close association we share.

My dad, Thomas Mecca, who is one of the wisest men I know. He had one of the greatest influences on my life. I am deeply grateful for his encouragement and his undying faith in me throughout the years.

My mother, Ann Mecca, who has departed from the planet and resides on a higher level. She was more than my mother. She was my friend and confidant. I miss her deeply but will always treasure the fun and activities we shared. I still rely on her teaching and advice.

My husband, Duane, who encourages me to go for my goals and allows me the time and space. He is most willing to take over my duties while I am in my office. He is the one who gives me comfort when I need it, and feeds me when I am hungry. He is the one who has confidence, and no matter what the trial, has been at my side for thirty-seven years, through the good and the lean. He is still, to this day, my husband, friend, and lover.

Our daughter, Luane, who keeps her mother young and vital by making her stretch her efforts and keep on challenging herself.

Ms. Mary Bruton of Soundria's Children's Services, who was one of the best, if not the best, administrators of the youth homes in which I was employed. She not only excelled in her field, but had deep sensitivity for both the children and the staff. She helped to further advance my techniques and had the ability to assist me on a personal level. I can still feel her strength and energy. I will always treasure her help and friendship.

Mr. Richard Tanski of Phoenix Printing, who encouraged my desire to write.

Sung In Printing America, and their staff, whose expertise in the final manifestation brought the message of the master to the world.

All of the children who have passed my way. They are the ones who enabled me to express my true passion of life through allowing me to interact with them.

Everyone who contributed their talents to the completion of this book, all my love. Thank You!

The intuitive force of nature, who firmly, but tenderly, sat me down in front of the word processor, and kept whispering to me, "Now, do it now. The world is ready and waiting for your message."

Footnotes

1   Jackson, Michael, *Moonwalk*, (New York: Doubleday, 1988); *all chapter quotes are taken from this reference, and the footnotes therefore are not repeated at the beginning quote of each chapter.*

2   *Michael Jackson Talks With Oprah* , ABC, February 10, 1993.

3a   *Moonwalk*

3b   *Moonwalk*, page 258

4   *Dangerous* CD Sleeve

5   *Dangerous* CD Cover

6   *Moonwalk*, page 181

7   *Moonwalk*, page 181

8   *Michael Jackson Talks With Oprah*

9   *Moonwalk*, page 174

10   *Moonwalk*, page 262-3

11   Life Magazine, June 1994, page 64

12   Life Magazine, page 56

13   *Moonwalk*, page 258

14   *Moonwalk*, pages 48-49, 258

15   *Moonwalk*, page 258

16   *Moonwalk*, pages 47-48

17   Life Magazine, page 64

18   Life Magazine, page 64

19   Jackson, Michael. *Dangerous, Gone Too Soon*

20   *Moonwalk*, page 204

21   *Moonwalk*, page 237

22   *Moonwalk*, page 244

23   *Moonwalk*, page 180
24   *Moonwalk*, page 224
25   *Moonwalk*, page 3
26   *Moonwalk*, page 159
27   *Moonwalk*, page 176
28   *Moonwalk*, pages 256-257
29   *Moonwalk*, page 196
30   *Moonwalk*, page 140
31   *Bad* Album, *Man in the Mirror*
32   *Michael Jackson Talks With Oprah*
33   *Moonwalk*, page 270
34   *Moonwalk*, page 244
35   *HIStory: Past, Present & Future, Book I* CD Insert
36   *HIStory: Past, Present & Future, Book I* CD Insert
37   *ABC PrimeTime with Diane Sawyer*, ABC, June 15, 1995
38   *ABC PrimeTime with Diane Sawyer*
39   Sandy Gallen, San Francisco Chronicle, June 15, 1995
40   *ABC PrimeTime with Diane Sawyer*
41   *The Complete Work of Michelangelo* (New York: Reynal & Company)
42   *HIStory: Past, Present & Future, Book I* CD Insert
43   *Moonwalk*, page 194
44   *Moonwalk*, page 195
45   *Moonwalk*, page 285
46   Labella, Vincenzo, *Season of Giants*, (New York: Little, Brown and Company 1990)